What Is Yet to Come

KAY ARTHUR
PETE De LACY

HARVEST HOUSE PUBLISHERS
EUGENE, OREGON

Scripture quotations are from the New American Standard Bible®, © 1960, 1962, 1963, 1968, 1971, 1972, 1973, 1975, 1977, 1995 by The Lockman Foundation. Used by permission. (www.Lockman.org)

Cover by Koechel Peterson & Associates, Inc., Minneapolis, Minnesota

WHAT IS YET TO COME
Copyright © 2011 by Precept Ministries International
Published by Harvest House Publishers
Eugene, Oregon 97402
www.harvesthousepublishers.com

Library of Congress Cataloging-in-Publication Data

Arthur, Kay
What is yet to come / Kay Arthur and Pete De Lacy.
    p. cm.—(The new inductive study series)
ISBN 978-0-7369-2833-5 (pbk.)
ISBN 978-0-7369-4022-1 (eBook)
1. Bible. O.T. Ezekiel—Textbooks. I. De Lacy, Pete. II. Title.
BS1545.55.A78 2011
224'.4007—dc22

                                                    2010028729

Printed in the United States of America

15 16 17 18 19 20 21 22 / BP-NI / 12 11 10 9 8 7 6 5 4 3

E 1-3
E 38-39
E 4-14
E 40-48
E 15-24
E 25-32
E 33-37

CONTENTS

∽∽∽∽

5

How to Get Started...

Reading directions is sometimes difficult and hardly ever enjoyable! Most often you just want to get started. Only if all else fails will you read the instructions. We understand, but please don't approach this study that way. These brief instructions are a vital part of getting started on the right foot and will help you immensely.

FIRST

As you study Ezekiel, you will need four things in addition to this book:

1. A Bible you are willing to mark in. The marking is essential. An ideal Bible for this purpose is *The New Inductive Study Bible (NISB)*. The *NISB* is in a single-column text format with large, easy-to-read type, which is ideal for marking. The margins of the text are wide and blank so you can take notes.

The *NISB* also has instructions for studying each book of the Bible, but it does not contain any commentary on the text, nor is it compiled from any theological stance. Its purpose is to teach you how to discern truth for yourself through the inductive method of study. (The various charts and maps that you will find in this study guide are taken from the *NISB*.)

Whichever Bible you use, just know you will need to mark in it, which brings us to the second item you will need...

2. A fine-point, four-color ballpoint pen or various colored fine-point pens that you can use to write in your Bible. Office supply stores should have these.

3. Colored pencils or an eight-color leaded Pentel pencil.

4. A composition book or a notebook for working on your assignments and recording your insights.

SECOND

1. As you study Ezekiel, you will be given specific instructions for each day's study. These should take you between 20 and 30 minutes a day, but if you spend more time than this, you will increase your intimacy with the Word of God and the God of the Word.

If you are doing this study in a class and you find the lessons too heavy, simply do what you can. To do a little is better than to do nothing. Don't be an all-or-nothing person when it comes to Bible study.

Remember, anytime you get into the Word of God, you enter into more intensive warfare with the devil (our enemy). Why? Every piece of the Christian's armor is related to the Word of God. And our one and only offensive weapon is the sword of the Spirit, which is the Word of God. The enemy wants you to have a dull sword. Don't cooperate! You don't have to!

2. As you read each passage in the Bible, train yourself to ask the "5 W's and an H": who, what, when, where, why, and how. Asking questions like these helps you see exactly what the Word of God is saying. When you interrogate the text with the 5 W's and an H, you ask questions like these:

What is the chapter about?

Who are the main characters?

When does this event or teaching take place?

Where does this happen?

Why is this being done or said?

How did it happen?

3. Locations are important in many books of the Bible, so marking references to these in a distinguishable way will be helpful to you. We double-underline every reference to a location in green (grass and trees are green!) using a four-color ballpoint pen. Some maps are included in the appendix so you can look up the locations.

4. References to time are also very important and should be marked in an easily recognizable way in your Bible. We mark them by putting a clock like this 🕐 in the margin of the Bible beside the verse where the phrase occurs. You may want to underline or color the references to time in one specific color.

5. You will be given certain key words to mark throughout this study. This is the purpose of the colored pencils and the colored pens. If you will develop the habit of marking your Bible in this way, you will improve your study significantly and will remember much more.

A key word is an important word that the author uses repeatedly in order to convey his message to his readers. Certain key words will show up throughout Ezekiel; others will be concentrated in specific chapters. When you mark a key word, you should also mark its synonyms (words that mean the same thing in the context) and any pronouns (*I, me, my, mine; you, your, yours; he, him, his; she, her, hers; it, its; we, us, our, ours; they, them, their, theirs…*) in the same way you marked the key word. Also, mark each word the same way in all of its forms (such as *judge, judgment,* and *judging*). We will give you a few suggestions for ways to mark key words in your daily assignments.

You can use colors or symbols or a combination of colors and symbols to mark words for easy identification. However, colors are easier to distinguish than symbols. When we use symbols, we keep them very simple. For example, you could draw a red heart around the word *love* and shade the inside of the heart like this: love.

When we mark the members of the Godhead (which we do not always do), we color each word yellow and mark *Father* with a purple triangle like this: **Father.** We mark *Son* this way: Son and *Holy Spirit* this way: Spirit.

Mark key words in a way that is easy for you to remember.

Devising a color-coding system for marking key words throughout your Bible will help you instantly see where a key word is used. To keep track of your key words, list them on a three-by-five card and mark them the way you mark them in your Bible. You can use this card as a bookmark.

6. A chart called EZEKIEL AT A GLANCE is included in the appendix. As you complete your study of a chapter, record the main theme of that chapter beside the appropriate chapter number. The main theme of a chapter is what the chapter deals with the most. It may be a particular subject or teaching.

If you will fill out the EZEKIEL AT A GLANCE chart as you progress through the study, you will have a synopsis of Ezekiel when you are finished. If you have a copy of *The New Inductive Study Bible*, you will find the same chart on pages 1401–1402. If you record your themes there, you will have them for a ready reference.

7. Always begin your study with prayer. As you do your part to handle the Word of God accurately, you must remember that the Bible is a divinely inspired book. The words that you are reading are truth, given to you by God so you can know Him and His ways more intimately. These truths are divinely revealed.

> For to us God revealed them through the Spirit;
> for the Spirit searches all things, even the depths

of God. For who among men knows the thoughts
of a man except the spirit of the man which is in
him? Even so the thoughts of God no one knows
except the Spirit of God (1 Corinthians 2:10-11).

Therefore ask God to reveal His truth to you as He leads and
guides you into all truth. He will if you will ask.

8. Each day when you finish your lesson, meditate on what
you saw. Ask your heavenly Father how you should live in light
of the truths you have just studied. At times, depending on how
God has spoken to you through His Word, you might even want
to write LFL ("Lessons for Life") in the margin of your Bible and
then, as briefly as possible, record the lesson for life that you
want to remember.

THIRD

This study is set up so that you have an assignment for every day of the week—so that you are in the Word daily. If you
work through your study in this way, you will benefit more
than if you do a week's study in one sitting. Pacing yourself
this way allows time for thinking through what you learn on a
daily basis!

The seventh day of each week differs from the other six
days. The seventh day is designed to aid group discussion;
however, it's also profitable if you are studying this book indi-
vidually.

The "seventh" day is whatever day in the week you choose
to finish your week's study. On this day, you will find a verse
or two for you to memorize and Store in Your Heart. Then
there is a passage to Read and Discuss. This will help you
focus on a major truth or major truths covered in your study
that week.

We have included Questions for Discussion or Individual Study to assist those using this book in a Sunday

school class or a group Bible study. Taking the time to answer these questions will help you apply the truth to your own life even if you are not doing this study with anyone else.

If you are in a group, be sure every member of the class, including the teacher, supports his or her answers and insights from the Bible text itself. Then you will be handling the Word of God accurately. As you learn to see what the text says and compare Scripture with Scripture, the Bible explains itself.

Always examine your insights by carefully observing the text to see what it *says*. Then, before you decide what the passage of Scripture *means*, make sure that you interpret it in the light of its context. Scripture will never contradict Scripture. If it ever seems to contradict the rest of the Word of God, you can be certain that something is being taken out of context. If you come to a passage that is difficult to understand, reserve your interpretations for a time when you can study the passage in greater depth.

The purpose of the THOUGHT FOR THE WEEK is to share with you what we consider to be an important element in your week of study. We have included it for your evaluation and, we hope, for your edification. This section will help you see how to walk in light of what you learned.

Books in the New Inductive Study Series are survey courses. If you want to do a more in-depth study of a particular book of the Bible, we suggest you do a Precept Upon Precept Bible study course on that book. You may obtain more information on these courses by contacting Precept Ministries International at 800-763-8280 or visiting our website at www.precept.org.

Ezekiel

INTRODUCTION TO EZEKIEL

In 622 BC, during the reign of King Josiah of Judah, the priests cleansing the temple found the book of the law. It had been ignored and eventually lost because of the idolatry of the preceding kings, priests, and people. According to the book of Deuteronomy, God told Israel that when the people had a king, he was to make a copy of the law and read it daily. Instead, nearly 800 years later, the Word of God was lost in the temple.

When young King Josiah learned about the book of the law, God's covenant with His people, and the nation's rightful response, he wept and tore his clothes in grief and anguish over Judah's awful sin. He knew God's wrath burned against the people's idolatry, and he determined to purge Judah of its idols, to change the culture of his day, and to lead the way in serving the Lord and keeping His commandments. He began a revival but didn't live to see it through, and the prophetess Huldah told Josiah that after his death God would bring judgment on Judah because they had forsaken Him. Idolatry was in their hearts despite the outward reforms of Josiah's reign.

God used Assyria to judge the northern kingdom—Israel, Judah's sister—removing its ten tribes from the promised land between 732 and 722 BC. Judah didn't learn from Israel's experience. Their idolatry continued, and they placed their trust in their military might, their political alliances, and their temple.

But Babylon was rising, replacing Assyria as the dominant power. Egypt tried to help Assyria against Babylon, and Josiah died in battle against Egypt. Egypt's Pharaoh deposed Josiah's son Jehoahaz after only three months' rule and placed another son, Eliakim, on the throne, changing his name to Jehoiakim and making Judah a puppet state.

But this was short-lived under the God who establishes kings and kingdoms. Babylon defeated Assyria and then pursued Egypt southward. When they came to Jerusalem in 605 BC, they made Jehoiakim *their* servant and took some young nobles captive, including Daniel and three friends we know as Shadrach, Meshach, and Abednego. Jehoiakim ruled until he died in 597 BC, and his son Jehoiachin took the throne.

The Babylonians returned to attack Jerusalem only three months into Jehoiachin's reign, taking him captive to Babylon with his wives, his mother, his officials, and a total of 10,000 people, including a young man named Ezekiel. As you'll see, Ezekiel is a priest who doesn't become 30 and thus eligible to serve in the temple until five years into his captivity in Babylon. In 586 BC, after the third siege of Jerusalem, the temple will be destroyed and not rebuilt for 70 years. Ezekiel may not serve as a priest in the temple in Jerusalem, but he will serve God as a prophet from Babylon, bringing God's message to the exiles— and to you and me.

In the appendix you'll find a chart called THE RULERS AND PROPHETS OF EZEKIEL'S TIME that will help you throughout your study of Ezekiel.

WATCHMAN
ON THE WALL

~~~~~

Is trouble brewing? Is danger ahead—something on the horizon that could spell disaster? God called Ezekiel to sound an alarm, to warn of impending doom, to save those who would repent at his warning. God warned Ezekiel of the consequences if he didn't give the warning and if the people didn't heed it. What about you? What will you do?

DAY ONE

When studying the Bible, the best way to begin is with prayer. Spiritual truth is spiritually discerned, so ask God to help you see and understand His truth through the Holy Spirit, who indwells all believers. We can teach you effective Bible study skills, but they aren't substitutes for prayer.

Read the first three verses of Ezekiel 1. What kind of book is this? You probably noticed that Ezekiel saw visions and that the word of the Lord came to him. These features characterize prophecy, so we're embarking on a study of prophecy—God's message about the future through a chosen spokesman. Remember that the prophet is simply the messenger; the message itself is from God.

When does the message come? Mark the references to

time with a distinctive color or a clock symbol. "The fifth year of King Jehoiachin's exile" must be 593 BC because the king was taken captive to Babylon in 597 BC along with Ezekiel and 10,000 others. Ancient cultures didn't begin their year in the winter, as we do, but in the spring, when new life begins, or in the fall, when the harvest is gathered. Refer to the chart called THE JEWISH CALENDAR in the appendix throughout your study.

Where is Ezekiel? The text says he is among the exiles by the river Chebar in the land of the Chaldeans. Chaldea is a region of Babylon. In the appendix, find the map called EXILES OF JUDAH TO BABYLON.

We've begun by asking the text some of the 5 W's and an H. We know *when, where,* and to *whom* the message was given. We even know something about the author—he's a priest. "The thirtieth year" most likely refers to his age—the year he would have been eligible to work in the temple as a priest according to Numbers 4:3.

But what's the message and who is it for? And why did God give this message? These questions will frame our study of Ezekiel's prophecy. We'll find the answers by looking at key repeated words and phrases—things the author emphasizes by repetition. You'll be marking many of these words and phrases throughout Ezekiel, so mark them on a three-by-five card the same way you'll mark them in the text, and use this card as a bookmark. Doing this as you go from chapter to chapter will help you mark consistently and save time.

You've already seen two phrases in the first three verses that are keys in the book—"the word of the LORD came" and "the hand of the LORD came upon him." You'll see variants of these too. Underline or shade each in a distinctive color throughout the book and put them on your bookmark.

Now read through the rest of Ezekiel 1. What happens in this chapter? What did Ezekiel see? What are the key figures?

Read through the chapter again and mark *living beings* (*creatures*), *wheel(s),* and the *one with the appearance of a man.* You don't need to add these to your bookmark because you won't see them throughout the book.

Take your time and drink in the scenery.

DAY TWO

If you're the type of person who enjoys pictures and likes to draw, see if you can sketch the characters in Ezekiel 1. Or perhaps you learn best by simply listing the features of each character. Choose your method and take your time. These are fantastic creatures, aren't they?

Now determine a theme for this chapter (what it's about) and record it on EZEKIEL AT A GLANCE in the appendix.

DAY THREE

Ezekiel 2 is only ten verses long, but it's important. The break between chapters 2 and 3 wasn't there in Ezekiel's day, so we're going to combine the chapters in our study today. Don't forget to begin your study time with prayer. (Remember, you have access to the Author, and He truly wants you to know, understand, and live by every word that comes from His mouth.) Then read through chapter 2 and focus on who is speaking to Ezekiel. From the context, determine whom the pronouns refer to. Also note what Ezekiel is called. Add this phrase to your bookmark and mark or color it distinctively. Also mark *listen*[1] and *rebellious.*

Now read through Ezekiel 3:1-11. Did you see whom the

message is for and how they're described? Make three lists in your notebook and record what you learn about the speaker, about Ezekiel, and about those he's sent to.

Now read Jeremiah 1:17-19 and Isaiah 6 and compare them with Ezekiel 2:6–3:11. What do you think about the prophet's task? Jeremiah and Ezekiel were contemporaries, and Isaiah prophesied before them both, so we can safely assume Ezekiel knew about God's call to Isaiah and Jeremiah and the difficulties they encountered.

List what you learned from marking *listen* and *rebellious*.

How do the difficulties these prophets faced challenge you with respect to the ministry God has given you as a member of the body of Christ?

Now determine the theme of Ezekiel 2 and record it on EZEKIEL AT A GLANCE in the appendix.

DAY FOUR

Let's pick up today where we left off yesterday in Ezekiel 3. We haven't asked you to mark references to *God* so far (sometimes there are just too many), but where you think they are significant, mark them. Some like to use a purple triangle shaded yellow for God the Father. You've already seen a couple of references to *the Spirit* so far, and now you'll see some more. You'll want to mark these in so you can come back later and list what you learn about the Spirit—what He does and how He operates.

Go back through Ezekiel 1:1-3 and 3:11 and mark the references to God.

Read Ezekiel 3:12-15, marking the key words from your bookmark. Note the location and the time phrase. As a general rule, we mark locations you can find on a map by double-underlining them in green.

What did you learn? Did you notice the reference to *the glory of the Lord*? This phrase appears early in the book and is worth marking. Go back to Ezekiel 1:28 and mark it there too.

DAY FIVE

Today read Ezekiel 3:16-27 and mark the key words and phrases from your bookmark. Also mark *warn, wicked,* and *iniquity (sin),* but don't add them to your bookmark.

List the watchman's responsibilities. What is he commanded to do and why? What are the consequences if he doesn't?

Read Genesis 9:5-6. How does this passage relate to Ezekiel 3?

Now read Acts 18:1-6 and 20:26-27. What do you think Paul was referring to in these passages? Do you see a connection with Ezekiel 3:17-21?

What two ways can men respond to the watchman's warning? What happens in each case? What happens to the watchman who does not warn a wicked man about his evil?

What does God tell Ezekiel to do in 3:22-27? Interrogate the text with the 5 W's and an H. Where does God command Ezekiel to go? What is Ezekiel to do? What does God tell him? What does Ezekiel see?

Think about these things and then record the theme of Ezekiel 3 on EZEKIEL AT A GLANCE.

DAY SIX

Let's spend today thinking about application. It's not enough for us to observe and understand the message God gave Ezekiel; we need to apply these truths today to our lives.

In fact, you can enhance your study by identifying lessons for life and recording them in a notebook, a journal, or the margin of your Bible.

So let's review Ezekiel 1. Ezekiel was a priest who didn't get to serve in the temple. How did he handle that? How did he respond to God's call on his life when it was different from what Moses' law said about the priesthood? What lesson can you learn for your life?

How serious is Ezekiel's calling, and how difficult will his mission be? Do you take God's call on your life as seriously?

When people reject God's Word—truth you've shared with them to help them avoid disaster—whom do they *ultimately* reject? How might this encourage you to persevere?

Do you see a parallel between the responsibilities of the watchman on the wall and evangelism today? If so, how does this motivate you to share the gospel?

Remember, all Christians are called to make disciples. Read Matthew 28:19-20 and meditate on it. Think about these things and go to the Father for strength to persevere in tough times. Ask Him to show you how to proceed in the environments He's placed you in.

Day Seven

 Store in your heart: Ezekiel 3:17
Read and discuss: Ezekiel 1–3

Questions for Discussion or Individual Study

∾ Discuss the setting of Ezekiel 1–3. Who is king of Judah, and what is the historical context?

- ∾ Discuss the vision. Focus on what is clear. If you have unanswered questions, note them for further study and discussion in later lessons.

- ∾ Discuss the concept of the watchman on the wall as it applies to your life.

- ∾ What did you learn about the Lord's call on Ezekiel that you can apply to your life?

- ∾ What did you learn about speaking God's message?

Thought for the Week

God called Ezekiel to be a watchman on the wall for the sake of His people. In ancient times such watchmen were guards or lookouts whose primary duty was keeping watch for and on anyone approaching their city. Usually they merely reported what they saw, and other authorities decided what to do. For example, in 2 Samuel 18:24-27, a watchman on the roof of a gate reports what he sees to King David. And even the ruling king can't guarantee what's going to happen: according to Psalm 127:1, "Unless the Lord guards the city, the watchman keeps awake in vain."

Ezekiel didn't stand watch on the physical wall of a physical city, but he performed the same duties. He watched for danger and reported it to God's people in exile. The danger is specific—when God declares that the wicked will die because of their iniquity, the watchman must warn the people.

God says that if the wicked turn from their wicked ways, they will live. But if Ezekiel fails to warn the wicked and they die in their sins, Ezekiel will be held guilty for their deaths. Although he does not personally kill them, his failure to warn them of the danger of persisting in wickedness is the same as killing them. Genesis 9:5-6 establishes the principle that God requires the life of those who kill a man, so this charge to

Ezekiel is not a new idea. It's rooted in the fact that man's life is sacred because God created him in His own image.

The charge is also rooted in the holiness of God and the holiness of God's people as His reflection—they are to be holy as He is holy. Thus, when God's people are wicked, they give unbelievers an incorrect vision of God. God's covenant people are to worship Him, and worship is a matter of how they live. Our lives demonstrate our worship of God.

So Ezekiel's mission as watchman was serious—a life-and-death matter. The consequence for shirking his duty was also serious—he would be guilty of the death of those who died in their sins because he didn't warn them. But there was a flip side to this consequence that was equally important. If Ezekiel warned the wicked and they ignored him and died in their sins, he was free of guilt for their death.

This is important to us because we're watchmen. The parallel is evangelism, or sharing the gospel with the lost. In the book of Romans, Paul says all sinned in Adam, and the wages of sin is death. The free gift of God is eternal life. So how is sharing this message parallel to Ezekiel's duty as watchman? If there's a danger associated with rejecting the gospel and we don't share it, we're guilty. So far as *our* guilt is concerned, it doesn't matter how people respond. That's not the watchman's responsibility. If they don't listen to us, we're free from guilt if they die in their sins.

Should our message extend beyond preaching the gospel to the lost? After all, God's charge to Ezekiel included warning the righteous ones who turn from their righteousness. Do God's people sometimes fall into sin? What is our responsibility to them? They too need to be warned and turned back from their evil way. They risk loss of reward, and the watchman bears guilt for not warning them to turn back to righteous living.

What does Ezekiel's example mean for you? Are you a watchman? Should you be? What is God telling you?

CAN YOU GET AWAY WITH IT?

∾∾∾∾

Does love overlook disobedience? If people really love you, will they let you get away with anything, or will they call you into account? God loves Judah—will He discipline them? God loves you—will He discipline you?

DAY ONE

We're going to cover four chapters this week. The pace will pick up a little bit, but we'll keep the homework load reasonable. Today read Ezekiel 4, marking the key words on your bookmark. Remember to keep asking the 5 W's and an H as you go.

Now, what two main things did God tell Ezekiel to do? In your notebook, list the specifics of each—build this, lie this way, and so forth. Now read over your list and ask the 5 W's and an H. Why is Ezekiel to do these things? How will these actions be a sign to Israel?

Read 2 Kings 25:1-3 and 2 Chronicles 36:11-21. What is coming in 586 BC and why? How do Ezekiel's signs to Israel relate to the coming events?

Also read Leviticus 22:1-8 and Deuteronomy 23:12-14.

How do these verses help you understand Ezekiel's concern about what he is to eat and how it will be prepared?

Finally, discern the theme of Ezekiel 4 and record it on EZEKIEL AT A GLANCE.

DAY TWO

The signs continue! Read Ezekiel 5 today, marking the key words and phrases from your bookmark.

Now list in your notebook what will happen to Judah and why. How does chapter 5 relate to chapter 4?

This chapter is prophecy. Remember that Ezekiel was taken captive in 597 BC and that this prophecy comes in 593 BC. The fulfillment will come in the siege of 586 BC. How certain is God's Word? Let's look at some cross-references to see. Read the following, taking pertinent notes.

Deuteronomy 28:49-57

Jeremiah 19:3-9

Lamentations 4:10

Deuteronomy was written before the Israelites entered the promised land. Jeremiah prophesied before and during the Babylonian sieges of Jerusalem, and Lamentations was written after the capture and destruction of Jerusalem and the temple.

What did you learn about God and His Word from the verses above?

Finally, thinking about all you have seen today, what's the main subject of Ezekiel 5? Record this theme on EZEKIEL AT A GLANCE.

Day Three

Read Ezekiel 6 and mark the key words on your bookmark. Mark references to idolatry such as *altars, high places,* and *idols.* Two additional words in Ezekiel 6 are important, but there's no need to add them to your bookmark because they're each used only once—*heart* and *remnant.*[2] List what you learned about the heart and the remnant.

Now let's look at some cross-references to expand our understanding of this chapter's message. The Old Testament refers to the remnant many times and in a variety of contexts. In Ezekiel 6, we learn that the coming destruction will not wipe out the remnant. Read Zechariah 8:6-13.

This is the key to understanding the concept of the remnant: God keeps the covenant He made with His chosen people Israel, so He will not make a complete end to them. A remnant will always remain but only through His purging, cleansing action. Not everyone will turn to Him. Read Zechariah 13:8-9.

Now read Ezekiel 6:9 again, consider the relationship God has with His people Israel, and then read the following cross-references:

> Deuteronomy 9:4-5
>
> Deuteronomy 10:12
>
> Deuteronomy 11:11-17
>
> Deuteronomy 30:1-6
>
> Jeremiah 31:31-33

Consider what God said through Ezekiel about the heart. We'll see much more about this subject later in Ezekiel. And just for a quick New Testament tidbit, read Colossians 3:5.

Finally, determine the theme of Ezekiel 6 and record it on EZEKIEL AT A GLANCE.

DAYS FOUR & FIVE

Ezekiel 7 is a bit longer, so we'll take two days to study it. Read chapter 7 and mark the words and phrases on your bookmark as usual. Mark *end* and its synonyms but don't add them to your bookmark. Remember, careful observation is the key to proper interpretation. You won't know what something means until you know what it says.

Now, list what you learned about the end. What will happen? To whom? Why? When will this occur? Take your time making this list. In the process, you may notice new key repeated words or phrases you'd like to go back and mark. That's normal. One thing leads to another as the picture becomes clearer.

Now think back over the message of Ezekiel 6 and the cross-references you looked up yesterday and before. Reread them if necessary. How does this message fit with all the rest?

Finally, record the theme of chapter 7 on EZEKIEL AT A GLANCE.

DAY SIX

As we did last week, let's use our last day to meditate on application to our own lives. Ezekiel's message was to his people, especially at that time, but it includes lessons for life for us today. First Corinthians 10:6 says these things happened as examples for us, for our instruction, and Romans 15:4 adds that they're recorded so we might have encouragement and hope. So when we study the Old Testament, we look for principles applicable to all times—timeless principles.

So let's look at God's judgments on ancient Israel to see how they relate to His relationship to the church today. Read the following verses:

Romans 14:10-12

1 Corinthians 11:31-32

2 Corinthians 5:10

Hebrews 9:27

Hebrews 12:4-11

1 Peter 4:17-18

Do you *expect* to be judged? How do judgment and discipline relate to each other? Why does a father discipline his children? Why does God discipline His children? How does this apply to your life here on earth?

It's been a full week, hasn't it? Praise the Lord for the opportunity to spend so much time with Him in His incomparable Word.

DAY SEVEN

 Store in your heart: Ezekiel 6:10

Read and discuss: Ezekiel 4:1-8; 5:1-13; 6:1-14; 7:1-4,14-22.

QUESTIONS FOR DISCUSSION OR INDIVIDUAL STUDY

- ∾ Describe each of the signs Ezekiel performed and then discuss the messages God intended to communicate through them.

- ∾ Discuss the justice of God's judgment on Israel. Describe what God expected from His people and what they did.

∾ What does God expect from us? What does He intend discipline to produce? How does His discipline of us differ from His discipline of Israel? How is it similar?

∾ What things in our lives today can be idols? Are there things you place before God? Leave time here for sharing.

Thought for the Week

Hebrews 12:4-11 reminds us that fathers express their love for their children by disciplining them. Children don't do everything their fathers tell them to do. We don't enjoy being disciplined, but the process is intended to correct us. Our earthly fathers want us to share the blessings of right living. They want us to develop the characteristics and habits that will lead to peaceful, enjoyable, productive lives.

If our earthly fathers know the heavenly Father, the principles they give us reflect our heavenly Father's principles. But many of us don't have earthly fathers who reflect our heavenly Father's love, wisdom, and character. What then?

The good news is that we all have the Father's Word to teach us His ways. That's what the Bible is—God's self-revelation to us. We have access to Him through the deposit of Scripture handed down to us by His holy servants, the authors of the 66 books of the Bible. We've got a sort of parenting manual, straight from the ultimate Father.

And what does our Father tell us? Expect discipline, chastening, and judgment on thoughts and actions that do not reflect His standards. The writer of Hebrews put it this way in 12:10: "They [our earthly fathers] disciplined us for a short time…but He disciplines us for our good, so that we may share His holiness."

Wow—we can share His holiness! God told Israel in Leviticus 11:45, "Be holy, for I am holy." Peter quoted this in 1 Peter 1:16 while explaining right behavior—how to live and how not to live. God wants us to share His holiness. That's pretty hard to grasp if you think about it very long. God's holiness is so far above ours, we can't completely comprehend sharing it.

But that's the good news. He helps us get to where we need to go, just as any good father would do. Through Jesus Christ's sacrifice, all our sins—past, present, and future, Adam's and ours—are put on Christ on the cross. "[God] made Him who knew no sin to be sin on our behalf, so that we might become the righteousness of God in Him" (2 Corinthians 5:21). And then God gave us a helper, the Holy Spirit, to empower us, teach us, and remind us of His ways.

But even though we have the best Teacher and the best instruction manual, we aren't perfectly obedient. We bear Adam's fallen nature and we sin, and this will continue until Jesus perfects us on His day (Philippians 1:6). So our loving heavenly Father, who wants us to share His holiness, disciplines us to show us the error of our ways and put us back on the path to holiness. He judges everything we do by filtering it through fingers of love.

God does this now. He gives us the things necessary to grow into the image of His Son, Jesus, in this life and in the next when we stand before Him. God judges perfectly. His judgments are completely just because He *is* just. He is also merciful, not giving us the punishment we deserve, and He's gracious, giving us the blessings we don't deserve. He is merciful and gracious in His love and discipline.

For these things, we can be eternally grateful.

Ichabod

೧೩೩೩

In the days of the judges, the Philistines fought against Israel and captured the ark of the covenant. Eli and his sons, Hophni and Phinehas—all three of them priests—died. Phinehas's wife was due to deliver a baby, and when she heard the terrible news, she went into labor and delivered a son, whom she named Ichabod ("no glory") because, she said, "The glory has departed from Israel." Many years later, King Solomon built a beautiful temple, and the glory of God filled it. Did the glory of God remain in Solomon's temple forever, or did it depart from Israel?

Day One

We're so thankful that you have decided to study God's Word for yourself, to learn His ways so you can stand firmly for Him in these difficult last days. The Bible says that we can expect difficult times, that men will reject truth, and that we must be ready at all times to declare truth—to defend the hope we have in us. Thank you for making yourself ready to share the truth.

Read Ezekiel 8:1 and mark the time phrase. Then compare it to the one you marked in Ezekiel 1:1-3. How much time has elapsed?

This time shift marks the beginning of a new subject and a new segment of the book—a common occurrence in historic and prophetic books of the Bible. New subjects usually bring new key words and phrases as well as new emphases on words you've seen before. As you study the next four chapters of Ezekiel, you should see this clearly.

Note what happens and where. Then read verse 2 and compare the first few words with Ezekiel 1:1. What happens here that is similar to chapter 1? How does this contrast with events in the last four chapters? What phrase did we see repeated in those chapters? (These changes also indicate a new subject and a new segment of the book.)

Read Ezekiel 8 today, marking the key words from your bookmark. Pay special attention to the phrase *the glory of the LORD*, which you saw earlier in the book. We double-underline geographical locations in green, but in this chapter the key locations in the vision are parts of the temple in Jerusalem. Choose a different method to mark these because they're keys to understanding this chapter.

In your notebook, describe briefly what Ezekiel saw. You might also want to make notes in the margins of your Bible.

Compare Ezekiel 8:2-4 with Ezekiel 1:26-28 and 3:23. What do you see?

Reread Ezekiel 8:5-18 and list in your notebook the location of the temple complex and what abomination Ezekiel saw. You might want to mark these in your Bible too. Refer to the diagram in the appendix called SOLOMON'S TEMPLE.

Now, who was involved in these abominations? How did God respond to the abominations? List the elements in your notebook.

DAY TWO

Let's do a little cross-referencing about abominations. Read Deuteronomy 32:15-32 and Jeremiah 7:30 and take pertinent notes in your notebook.

Let's also explore the heritage of Shaphan by reading the following about some of his descendants.

> 2 Kings 22:3-12
>
> Jeremiah 26:24
>
> Jeremiah 36:10-12
>
> Jeremiah 39:14

Finally, record the theme of Ezekiel 8 on EZEKIEL AT A GLANCE.

DAY THREE

Today we're going to dig into events in Ezekiel 9 that are tied to events in Ezekiel 8. Read the chapter and mark key words and phrases from your bookmark as well as locations just as you have before. As you read and mark, remember to ask all the pertinent 5 W's and an H questions you can think of. Remember what you learned from Ezekiel 8 as you go.

Note who was spared, who was slain, and why. How did Ezekiel react? How did the Lord respond to Ezekiel? Remember, this vision (like all visions) contains a message.

What is the significance of the man clothed in linen? Read the following verses:

> Daniel 10:4-6
>
> Daniel 12:5-7

Revelation 15:6

Revelation 19:7-16

Marking certain groups is beneficial elsewhere in Scripture. Look up the following references and compare them to Ezekiel 9. What do you learn?

Exodus 12:1-13

2 Corinthians 1:21-22

Ephesians 1:13-14

Revelation 7:2-3; 9:1-4; 14:1-5

Has God given this message before? Read Jeremiah 5:1-3.

How do Ezekiel 8 and 9 relate? Read Deuteronomy 17:2-7 and compare it with Ezekiel 8:16-17 and 9:4-6.

Determine a theme for Ezekiel 9 and record it on EZEKIEL AT A GLANCE.

DAY FOUR

After you pray, read Ezekiel 10 and mark key words and phrases from your bookmark.

List items that describe the cherubim and the wheels. Compare this to your list of descriptions of the living beings from chapter 1. Making a two-column chart and matching up characteristics will help a lot. If you're artistic, you could even draw a sketch. If you're not artistic, don't even think about it! Just enjoy comparing notes with the other members of your discussion group.

How do chapters 1 and 10 relate to each other?

What do you see in this chapter that you can apply to your life? Is there a truth about God you haven't seen before or something else that might encourage you to fall down in worship?

Finally, determine a theme for Ezekiel 10 and record it on EZEKIEL AT A GLANCE.

DAYS FIVE & SIX

Read Ezekiel 11 and mark key words and phrases as before. Don't miss geographical references. Then list what you learn about what happens to the people and the city.

Compare Ezekiel 11:13 to Ezekiel 9:8. What's the connection?

What is the message in Ezekiel 11:14-21? How does it relate to what you've seen so far in this vision? How does it answer Ezekiel's question? Compare Jeremiah 31:31-40.

Note what happens to the glory of the God of Israel in verses 22-23. Go back through chapters 8–11 and write down in your notebook what you learn about the glory of God. Pay particular attention to the locations. Tuck that information away in your memory because we'll come back to this in later chapters.

Now determine a theme for Ezekiel 11 and record it on EZEKIEL AT A GLANCE. Then thank God for His help this week as you've studied, and ask Him to continue teaching you in the coming week.

DAY SEVEN

 Store in your heart: Ezekiel 11:19
Read and discuss: Ezekiel 8–11

QUESTIONS FOR DISCUSSION OR INDIVIDUAL STUDY

- ∾ Discuss what the people had done in the temple.

- ∾ Review what you learned about the glory of the Lord in this week's lesson.

- ∾ Why did God leave the temple?

- ∾ Discuss what you've learned so far about Israel's idolatry and God's previous efforts to get the nation's attention.

- ∾ What did you learn about the cherubim?

- ∾ Discuss the man in linen, the marking, and the slaughter.

- ∾ What application can you make to your own life from these events?

THOUGHT FOR THE WEEK

The glory of the Lord first appeared to Israel when they set out on their journey from Egypt to the promised land. The Lord went before Israel in a pillar of cloud by day and a pillar of fire by night, and the glory of the Lord appeared again on Mount Sinai. The glory of the Lord filled the tabernacle when it was built and Solomon's temple in Jerusalem when it was dedicated. This visible manifestation is often called the *Shekinah* (the modern Hebrew word for "cloud of glory"). The Shekinah reminded Israel that He dwelt among them. In the temple, it rested in the Most Holy Place above the mercy seat, which covered the ark of the covenant.

Long before the temple was built, when Israel finished their wilderness wandering and began to enter the promised land, they carried the ark with them in their first battle at Jericho.

Because of their success at Jericho, the Israelites assumed that if they brought the ark to other battlefields, God again would be with them—because His presence was in the ark.

But 1 Samuel 4–6 tells a different story. After Israel was more or less established in the promised land but before the temple was built, the Israelites and Philistines fought, and the Philistines prevailed. The Israelites thought the Lord had defeated them because they did not have the ark with them, so they brought the ark from Shiloh to the camp. Their worship had turned to superstition, and they treated the ark like a pagan idol.

The Israelite army camp rejoiced when the ark came into their camp because they thought God was now in their midst and they would win the battle. To their horror, the Philistines not only won the battle but also captured the ark. The disaster was memorialized in the name of the priest's orphaned grandson, Ichabod (1 Samuel 4:22).

The ark brought nothing but trouble for the Philistines, so they returned it to Israel. Many years later, when it was placed in Solomon's temple, the glory of the Lord so filled the temple that the priests could not stand in its presence to minister. But after that, God's presence in the temple was not mentioned in Scripture until Ezekiel.

And what do we find in Ezekiel? A temple filled with idolatry. This was not new. Israel had become idolatrous in the days of Solomon and remained so from the days of his son Rehoboam to the days of Ezekiel, when Rehoboam's descendant Zedekiah sat on the throne of David. Several kings between these two instituted reforms, knowing that God's glory and idol worship could not exist together. Their solution was to rid the land of idols and cleanse the temple. Those kings were right. God does not share His glory with other so-called gods.

But the people's hearts were never cleansed of idolatry, so God made the ultimate separation—He left the temple, and

He left Jerusalem. Despite His promise in 2 Chronicles 7:16 that His *name* and His *eyes and heart* would be there perpetually, He did not promise His *presence* would remain forever. He tells Israel in the rest of the chapter that if they fall into idolatry, He will take them out of the land and make the land and the house a proverb and byword among other peoples, and they will know that these judgments came because they abandoned Him.

Fast-forward to Ezekiel's day. The judgments are about to happen, and God sends Ezekiel to remind His people one more time. This vision occurs just six years before the temple and Jerusalem are destroyed. With no temple, God's glory will not be there.

Seventy years later the temple will be rebuilt by those who return from Babylon, but they know it will not have the glory of Solomon's temple. Still, God tells them to take courage because a day will come when He will fill His house with an even greater glory.

The glory has departed, but it will not stay away forever. A day will come with not just restored glory but also better glory, a day in which peace will reign. No longer will God's people say "Ichabod—the glory has departed," but rather "Jehovah-Shammah—the Lord is there."

IDOLS IN THE HEART

∿∿∿∿

The princes, prophets, and elders of Israel were not effective role models. They were leaders, but they led the people astray. They corrupted the people with their bad examples and put stumbling blocks in the path of those who sought to worship and obey God. They had idols in their hearts, so they made idols with their hands. What will happen to them?

DAY ONE

Keep up the good work! We're so proud of you for wanting to study God's Word and following through! Let's start this week by reading Ezekiel 12:1-16 and marking key words and phrases from your bookmark.

List in your notebook the features of the sign in these verses and the message the sign is supposed to deliver. What should the people realize and how?

Now let's do some cross referencing about these events. Read these verses:

2 Kings 25:1-7

2 Chronicles 36:11-21

Jeremiah 32:2-5

How faithful is God to His Word? How precisely are His prophecies fulfilled?

What key phrase in Ezekiel 12:15-16 is the underlying principle for all God swears to do to Judah, Jerusalem, the temple, and Zedekiah the king? What does this tell you about things that happen in your life?

DAY TWO

Read Ezekiel 12:17-28 and mark the key words and phrases on your bookmark.

Now list in your notebook what you learned from marking these key words. What is Ezekiel called to do and why? What message will his action convey?

How far in the future is the fulfillment of this prophecy? What was the house of Israel saying?

What does this account tell you about people's response to biblical prophecy today? What is the danger of assuming that prophecy won't be fulfilled for many years?

Now determine the theme of Ezekiel 12 and record it on EZEKIEL AT A GLANCE.

Finally, Beloved, what is God's lesson for us? What can we apply to our lives?

DAY THREE

Read and mark Ezekiel 13:1-16 today. Then list in your notebook what you learned.

Has this "false prophecy" been spoken before? Read Jeremiah 5:12; 14:13-15; 23:16-22,30-32.

What had God told Israel about false prophets in general before? Read Deuteronomy 13:1-5 and 18:15-22.

What is consistent about God's response to these false prophets?

DAY FOUR

Read and mark Ezekiel 13:17-23 today. Then list in your notebook what you learned about the false prophets and those who sew magic bands on their wrists.

God had dealt with divination before. Read Deuteronomy 18:10-14 and 1 Samuel 15:23. What do we deal with today? Read 2 Timothy 4:3-4 and 2 Peter 2:1-3.

Compare Ezekiel 13:22 with Ezekiel 3:17-21. What do you learn?

Discern the theme of Ezekiel 13 and record it on EZEKIEL AT A GLANCE.

DAY FIVE

Read Ezekiel 14:1-11 and mark the key words on your bookmark. List what you learn from marking *idols* and *hearts*.

What were those with idols in their hearts doing, and how did the Lord respond to them? What does God want them to do? What will God do if they don't repent? Why does He do this?

Does God discipline those who approach Him improperly today? Read Acts 5:1-11 and 1 Corinthians 11:27-32.

DAY SIX

Read Ezekiel 14:12-23 and mark the key words on your bookmark. Then read verses 13-20 again and list what happens when a country sins. What's the connection to Israel? What phrase in verse 21 connects the two?

What do you know about the righteousness of Noah, Job, and Daniel? Read Genesis 6:9; Job 1:1,22; 2:10; and Daniel 1:8,17-21. In Ezekiel 14:14-20, what does God say about these men's righteousness? Whom can they save? Can a man save another man?

What do you learn about *comfort* in verses 21-23? What fear or question did Ezekiel have earlier when God showed him the judgment on Judah?

What is the answer? Comfort and compassion are related concepts. What did you learn about God's character that will help you in difficult times? Remember, we're studying the Bible to learn not only about other people but also about how we should live to the glory of God.

Don't forget to record the theme of Ezekiel 14 on EZEKIEL AT A GLANCE.

DAY SEVEN

 Store in your heart: Ezekiel 14:20
Read and discuss: Ezekiel 12:1-16; 13:1-14

QUESTIONS FOR DISCUSSION OR INDIVIDUAL STUDY

∾ Discuss the sign about baggage and its fulfillment. What did you learn about God?

ꙮ What did you learn about true and false prophets?

ꙮ How does God view divination? What parallels are there today?

ꙮ What are some examples of idols in the heart, and how do they affect people?

ꙮ Discuss how countries sin against God. What does this mean for your country?

ꙮ How does God's comfort and compassion relate to His judgments?

THOUGHT FOR THE WEEK

When Jesus told His disciples about His impending crucifixion, Peter protested that it should not happen. Jesus' response is instructive. He called Peter a stumbling block because he was not setting his mind on God's interests but man's.

Similarly, God told Ezekiel to tell Israel that those who set up idols in their hearts put the stumbling block of their iniquity right before their faces. And if they come to the prophet to inquire of the Lord, the Lord will answer according to the multitude of their idols. They must put them away and return to God.

Idols are anything we worship before God. Colossians 3:5 says greed is idolatry. The greatest commandment is to love Him with all our heart, soul, mind, and strength, and the Ten Commandments begin with a directive to have no other gods before Him. We are to love God above all else.

A stumbling block is anything that keeps us from God's interests. First Corinthians 1:23 says "Christ crucified" is a stumbling block to Jews. So while one stumbling block is anything that keeps us from coming to God in the first place, another one is anything that keeps us from following God fully, from achieving maturity as Christians.

Liberty can be a stumbling block to those who are weak in their faith, and so even our perfectly moral interests can cause people to stumble. We don't see these as idols in our hearts, but if something we're permitted to do is more important to us than our brothers' faith, isn't it an idol? It is certainly self-interest, not God's. So we must challenge ourselves to think beyond idols to the self-interests that can be stumbling blocks—even our freedom.

Paul addressed several examples. In 1 Corinthians 8 he talked about freedom to eat food sacrificed to idols. But if this freedom causes a believer to stumble, should we do it? The ultimate question is this: Do we care more about ourselves than we do about our brother? Do we have God's interests at heart, or our own?

Paul echoes this in Romans 14 when he explains that the kingdom of God is not food or drink, so we should not let these things become stumbling blocks to those whose faith is weak. The principle at stake is selflessness—setting aside our rights, privileges, desires, and freedoms, and acting for the good of our brothers and sisters.

Remember that this is the model we have in Christ. The great *kenosis* passage of Philippians 2 tells us that Christ humbled Himself to the point of becoming a servant, obedient to the point of death on a cross for the interests of others.

For this God exalted Him. This is what Jesus calls us to—radical humility, radical selflessness, taking up our crosses and following Jesus, following His example in all things.

We should have no idols in our hearts, nothing between us and God, nothing of self-interest. All to Jesus. All to God's interest.

WHAT HAPPENS TO HARLOTS?

∾∾∾∾

God likens Israel's idolatry to harlotry. He took Israel to be His bride, but she left Him to follow many other lovers—idols and gods from other nations. Did these other lovers really love her, or did they turn on her and destroy her? Contrast these gods' loyalty to Israel with God's true love for Israel, which is reflected in His covenant. And then consider what all this has to do with your own relationship with God.

DAY ONE

Remember that God the Holy Spirit is our Teacher, so beginning your study with prayer is critical. After you pray, read Ezekiel 15 and mark the key words and phrases on your bookmark.

List the comparisons God makes between the wood of the vine and the inhabitants of Jerusalem. What main point is He making?

Record the theme of Ezekiel 15 on EZEKIEL AT A GLANCE.

DAYS TWO THROUGH FIVE

Ezekiel 16 is a very long chapter, so we'll take four days to cover it. The observations alone will take a while, so pace yourself. Don't get worn out as you read, mark, and ask questions. Soak in the story that unfolds. Anytime you need to stop and review what you've read to keep the story straight, do so. It helps to make notes in the margins of your Bible paragraph by paragraph.

So dig in, faithful student. Read Ezekiel 16 and mark the key words and phrases from your bookmark. Also mark references to *Jerusalem, covenant,* and *harlots.*[3] You'll see *covenant* is prominent in this chapter and the next, so add it to your bookmark. *Covenant* is a key word throughout the Bible, so we recommend always marking it. *Harlotry* is key in this chapter and chapter 23, so we'll let you decide whether to add it to your bookmark.

Don't get overwhelmed by all the pronoun references to Jerusalem. If it's too much marking, don't do it. But you'll see how key Jerusalem is in this chapter.

Now list in your notebook the basic story of Jerusalem from its birth. Remember to keep asking the 5 W's and an H.

Make a separate list of Jerusalem's harlotries, unless you did so in your list of the basic story (you may just have written "committed harlotry"). How does this list relate to the message of chapter 15?

Hosea, the last prophet to the northern kingdom of Israel, was given a message about harlotry. Read Hosea 1–2 for the message and its tone (Hosea is 14 chapters long). Notice the parallels to Ezekiel's message to Judah.

Who are Jerusalem's sisters, and why are they mentioned?

A synecdoche is a literary device in which part of something is cited to represent the whole (or vice versa). For example, "fifty sails" can refer to "fifty boats."

In this passage, do the capital cities of Jerusalem and

Samaria represent all of Judah and Israel? In other words, are the messages in this chapter directed only to the occupants of the cities, or do they extend to the entire populations of the kingdoms of Judah and Israel? Remember the historical context of Ezekiel—the things he's seen in the visions and who he's directed to give them to.

The rampant idolatry of Jerusalem and Samaria is portrayed throughout 1 and 2 Kings, but for a snapshot, read 1 Kings 16:29-33 and 2 Kings 8:16-19.

Why does Ezekiel introduce Sodom as Jerusalem's younger sister?

What covenants are referred to? You've read Jeremiah 31:31-34 before, but refresh your memory if you need to.

Finally, when you've absorbed all you can from this chapter, record a theme for Ezekiel 16 on EZEKIEL AT A GLANCE.

Day Six

Observe Ezekiel 17, marking key words from your bookmark. Mark *Babylon* but don't add it to your bookmark. You should notice four paragraphs—the first two contain a parable, the third provides the explanation, and the last introduces a new but related subject.

List the basics of the parable in your notebook. You might want to make a two-column chart, the left column for facts of the parable and the right column for explanations.

This parable (which predicts future events) refers to Nebuchadnezzar and Zedekiah. Read 2 Kings 24:8–25:7 for the historical context.

How does this relate to the last paragraph of Ezekiel 17? What can we learn from it?

Finally, determine a theme for Ezekiel 17 and record it on EZEKIEL AT A GLANCE.

DAY SEVEN

 Store in your heart: Ezekiel 16:62
Read and discuss: Ezekiel 15; 16:1-22,30-34,36-37,41-43,60-63; 17:11-24

QUESTIONS FOR DISCUSSION OR INDIVIDUAL STUDY

- ⚮ Discuss your insights about the wood of the vine and the trees of the forest.

- ⚮ Review the story of Jerusalem's birth and adoption.

- ⚮ How did Jerusalem repay God's favor?

- ⚮ What will be the consequences for harlotry?

- ⚮ How is Jerusalem's harlotry unique?

- ⚮ What is the relationship between Sodom, Samaria, and Jerusalem?

- ⚮ Do these cities represent nations? If so, how?

- ⚮ What is the final glorious promise to Jerusalem?

- ⚮ What have you learned that you can apply to your life?

THOUGHT FOR THE WEEK

The language of Ezekiel 16 is graphic and explicit but poignant. Ezekiel provides a new dimension to the special relationship between God and His people (and especially Jerusalem). The story of finding a baby in a field, bringing it into a home, and raising it adds an aspect of intimacy rarely found in the

Old Testament. Watching the child grow, become a wife, and then play the harlot is heartbreaking.

Harlot is a somewhat archaic term. We don't use it much today; words like *prostitute* and *whore* are more common. And Ezekiel's account shows that Jerusalem's behavior has sunk to unprecedented depths. Instead of demanding pay for her illicit services, she actually paid others to be her lovers!

What is God's reaction to this? Despair? No—He is enraged! Remember, one of God's names is *Qanna*—"Jealous" (Exodus 34:14). Strictly speaking, jealousy is not wanting to share something you have with another. Dictionaries sometimes equate jealousy with envy, and we use the words interchangeably, but we must make a distinction when referring to God. He does not envy anyone. Envy is wanting something someone else has. God says He's jealous, not envious. He created all things, and all things belong to Him, so He can't be envious of anyone. Israel is His wife. He is jealous for her and does not want to share her with idols, or so-called gods. Her harlotry with them is an abomination that enrages Him.

So what does the God of the universe do when He is infuriated by His wife's adultery? He exposes her duplicity ("nakedness") to her lovers, who in turn stone her, burn her houses, and cut her to pieces with the sword. Then she stops paying her lovers, and God's anger abates.

Israel will not get away with harlotry—it is no secret to God. And we can't get away with it either for the same reason. God knows when we worship idols. And He will expose our harlotry and use these "lovers" to judge us. All sin has consequences. Sometimes, people may seem to be getting away with something, but the appearance lasts only for a season. The day of reckoning will come. We all will stand before the judgment seat of Christ and give an account. And the lost will stand before the great white throne. We are all judged by the one true, impartial, totally just, all-knowing God.

But there's hope in this. God is a covenant-keeping God. Those who are included in His new covenant have the promise of eternal life despite their sins. He disciplines us only to correct us, to refine us, and to make us holy so we can blamelessly stand before Him. We will not get away with our sins; we will give an account. But the God who judges is also merciful. We will suffer consequences, including loss of reward, but because of His mercy in Christ Jesus, we are His forever. We may be struck down, but we will be not destroyed. We have a sure hope because we are sealed with the Holy Spirit, the pledge of our inheritance in Christ Jesus (Ephesians 1:13-14). The promise to Jerusalem in Ezekiel 16:60-62 extends to all who believe the gospel of Jesus Christ. We have an everlasting covenant with the covenant-keeping God, and we will know Him.

THAT YOU MAY KNOW THAT I AM THE LORD YOUR GOD

❧❧❧❧

God told Ezekiel He would do certain things so Israel would never forget He is their God. Israel may not expect or want these things, but they will demonstrate God's sovereignty. God's people must learn that they are not in ultimate control, masters of their own fates, lords of their own lives. They belong to God, and when they rebel, He will act.

DAY ONE

Read Ezekiel 18:1-18 today, marking key words and phrases from your bookmark. You might want to mark *righteous(ness)*[4] in this chapter, but don't add it to your bookmark.

List things that are punishable by death.

Now, what is the main point of these verses? Compare this with Deuteronomy 5:9-10 and 24:16. What did the Law say? How does the Law differ from the proverb? By the way, did you notice who's judged in Deuteronomy 5:9-10?

Compare Genesis 15:6, Habakkuk 2:4, and Romans 1:17. What do you learn?

Remember, compare Scripture with Scripture—it contains no contradictions. If one passage *seems* to disagree with another, the problem is that we don't fully understand.

DAY TWO

We'll finish observing Ezekiel 18 today. Read Ezekiel 18:19-32 and mark the key words from your bookmark. Also mark *wicked* but don't add it to your bookmark.

Compare with Ezekiel 3:17-21. What does God desire? (Note: *Turn, turn away,* and *repent* are all translations of the same Hebrew word.)

Has God's desire changed? What did Jesus preach? Read Matthew 4:17.

What was wrong with Israel's understanding of the Law? What phrase starts Ezekiel 18:19, 25, and 29?

Compare Ezekiel 18:31 with Ezekiel 11:19. What do you learn?

Finally, determine a theme for Ezekiel 18 and record it on EZEKIEL AT A GLANCE.

DAY THREE

After beginning in prayer, read Ezekiel 19, marking the key words and phrases from your bookmark. Pay close attention to the two metaphors in this lament.

List what you learn about the lions and cubs in verses 1-9, and then make a second list of what you learn about the vine in verses 10-14. Both are about a mother.

Who are the lions and cubs? From your study of Kings and Chronicles and any historical charts, can you see what the cubs that became lions are?

What is the vineyard? Read Isaiah 5:1-7. What does the imagery of Ezekiel 19:10-14 tell you?

Record a theme for Ezekiel 19 on EZEKIEL AT A GLANCE.

DAY FOUR

As usual we'll read and mark the words and phrases from your bookmark. Today we'll cover Ezekiel 20:1-26, and tomorrow we'll finish the chapter.

Note the time phrase in verse 1 and compare it to the time phrase in Ezekiel 8:1. Also make sure to mark references to locations.

Read Exodus 5:1–6:9 and Acts 7:35-43 for a refresher on Israel's rebellion in Egypt. While Israel was in Egypt, how did they react to God, and what did He initially resolve to do to them there (Ezekiel 20:8)? But what did He actually do (verses 9-10)?

In your notebook, create a list or a chart like the one below and fill in the blanks. Do you see a general pattern?

What God said	How Israel responded	What God resolved to do	What God actually did and why
20:11-12:			
	20:13a:		
		20:13b:	
			20:14:
		20:15-16:	
			20:17:
20:18-20:			
	20:21a:		
		20:21b:	
			20:22:

Read Exodus 32:1-14 and Numbers 14:1-23 for more information about Israel's rebellion in the wilderness.

As you've discovered, Ezekiel 20 mentions several times that Israel profaned the Sabbath. What is the Sabbath for? Read Genesis 2:1-3 and Exodus 31:13. Compare with Hebrews 4:1-10.

DAY FIVE

Complete your observations of Ezekiel 20 by reading and marking verses 27-49. Note the first word of verse 27 and remember that what follows is based on what preceded—that's what *therefore* tells you.

List items that describe Israel's current condition. Also list items that describe their future. Why does God promise this—what's the key repeated phrase for the ultimate purpose for His actions?

What happens in verse 45? What are the geographical references there? Who will see that the Lord has acted?

Does Israel believe Ezekiel?

Finally, discern the theme of chapter 20 and record it on EZEKIEL AT A GLANCE.

DAY SIX

For our last study day this week, read Ezekiel 21 and mark the key words and phrases from your bookmark as you have been doing.

Note the people addressed. What will happen to them? Who will know why this has happened?

What did you learn about the sword?

What will the king of Babylon do?

Now read verse 27 again and meditate on it. Who is "He whose right it is," to whom God will give the ruin?

Who else is judged in this chapter beside Israel? Why are they judged by the sword?

Read Genesis 19:29-38 for Ammon's origin. Then read Deuteronomy 23:1-6 to discover the reason for God's animosity toward them.

Don't forget our last step—to record the chapter theme for Ezekiel 21 on EZEKIEL AT A GLANCE.

DAY SEVEN

 Store in your heart: Ezekiel 20:12

Read and discuss: Ezekiel 18:19-32; 19:1-9; 20:27-44; 21:1-17,27

QUESTIONS FOR DISCUSSION OR INDIVIDUAL STUDY

- ∞ Discuss the principle of bearing guilt.

- ∞ What does God desire? What do *turn away* and *repent* mean? Does God want these things from us?

- ∞ What did you learn about the kings of Israel from the metaphor of the cubs and lions?

- ∞ How was Israel like the nations, and how did God react to them?

- ∞ Describe and discuss God's mercy toward Israel after He judged them (chapter 20).

- ∞ What was the purpose of the sword? How did God use it for Israel?

- ∞ What hope does Israel have in the face of judgment and destruction?

THOUGHT FOR THE WEEK

One of the reasons God chose Israel was to show the world what He is like and what His people are to be like—holy, as He is. One key function of the Law given at Mount Sinai was to describe holy behavior.

But Israel failed the standards. They acted like the nations around them, first by asking for a king as the other nations did (rejecting God as their king) and then by adopting the gods and worship practices of the nations, rejecting God as their God. Israel did not show the world what holiness was—how God's people should act.

Although Israel broke the covenant God established with them, God kept it. God had opportunities to eradicate the majority of the nation and make a new one. He said as much to Moses and offered to make a new nation out of him. But God acted for His name's sake. Rather than create the impression that He led the people out of Egypt to destroy them, He relented. He kept His covenant by disciplining them, purging out the worst idolaters. He showed them that He is God—*their* God.

The repeated phrase in Ezekiel—"you will know that I am the LORD"—means God will demonstrate to Israel that *He* is Lord and the worthless idols of the nations are not. He will demonstrate that He is the sovereign ruler of the universe and of all nations, the self-existent one, the great I AM who revealed Himself to Moses and Israel and made a covenant with them.

He also intends to show that He is Judge of all flesh: "All flesh will see that I, the LORD, have kindled it" (referring to the fire in the forests of the Negev). "All flesh will know that I, the LORD, have drawn the sword out of its sheath" (referring to the judgment on Israel).

The judgments on Israel were not only for Israel's benefit but also for the sake of all mankind. They show the world that

God loves Israel enough to purify them and then, after disciplining them, to bring them back to the land He promised Abraham.

God used Babylon as the instrument of His judgment, but He still intended for all men to know that He, not the king of Babylon, judged Israel.

Our role as the church is similar to Israel's. We too are to show the world who God is in the person of His Son, Jesus. After the Last Supper, Jesus prayed that the world would believe and know that God sent Him and that God loves the church as He loves His Son. The world will know this through the perfect unity of the church with itself ("they may be one") and with the Father and Son ("they may be one in us.")

Jesus is the Light of the world, and so are we because He is in us and we are in Him. The world sees Jesus through us as we shine His light and dispel darkness. This is how He rescues men from the kingdom of darkness.

THE WRATH OF GOD

∾∾∾∾

Refiners use fire to purify metals. They heat the metal so impurities will rise to the surface for separation. Pure metal is the result. Fire is also used to destroy—it can burn things that are harmful to others so that new life can spring up. God's wrath purifies His people by destroying things that hurt them, and new life blossoms.

DAYS ONE & TWO

We're covering three chapters this week, taking two days of study for each, so the pace will be a bit more relaxed today and tomorrow. Start by observing Ezekiel 22, marking the words and phrases on your bookmark. Ask the 5 W's and an H as you go. Remember to always interrogate the text and read with a purpose.

Pay attention to the characters described. Make lists of what you learn about each group: rulers, priests, princes, prophets, and people. Then list what you learned about what God will do and why. Note the imagery of metals and dross.

Read Psalm 66:10, Isaiah 48:10, Daniel 12:10, and Zechariah 13:9 for more references to God refining.

What did you learn about refining metal that you can use in your own life? Does God refine us to remove impurities? Read Titus 2:11-14 and then meditate on how God is working in you.

Record a theme for Ezekiel 22 on EZEKIEL AT A GLANCE.

DAYS THREE & FOUR

Read Ezekiel 23 and mark the key words and phrases from your bookmark. Mark each reference to the two sisters but don't add them to the bookmark. Also mark the nations to whom these sisters turned. Take your time as you read and mark this long chapter, and remember to ask 5 W's and an H as you go.

Outline what will happen to Oholibah and why.

Finally, determine a theme for Ezekiel 23 and record it on EZEKIEL AT A GLANCE.

Think about what you have learned. What truth can you apply to your life?

DAYS FIVE & SIX

Read Ezekiel 24, marking key words and phrases. Note the time phrase in verse 1 and compare it to the time phrase in Ezekiel 20:1.

How long has Ezekiel been prophesying? What event happens in this year? According to THE RULERS AND PROPHETS OF EZEKIEL'S TIME (in the appendix), in how many years will Jerusalem be destroyed?

Reread the parable of the pot and list in your notebook what will happen to Jerusalem. Remember, a parable has a central message, so individual details of the parable can be *true* without being as *significant* as the main point.

How will Ezekiel be a sign to Jerusalem? What will Jerusalem know?

Finally, record a theme for Ezekiel 24 on EZEKIEL AT A GLANCE.

DAY SEVEN

 Store in your heart: Ezekiel 22:30
Read and discuss: Ezekiel 22:1-12,17-31; 23:1-28,46-49; 24:1-24

QUESTIONS FOR DISCUSSION OR INDIVIDUAL STUDY

- ∾ Discuss the abominations of the rulers, priests, prophets, princes, and people.

- ∾ What did you learn from the imagery of dross?

- ∾ What judgment will God's people receive and why?

- ∾ Discuss Oholah and Oholibah—whom they represent, what they've done, and the consequences of their actions.

- ∾ What did you learn about Israel from the parable of the pot?

- ∾ Discuss the sign Ezekiel will be.

- ∾ What application can you make from these chapters?

THOUGHT FOR THE WEEK

One of the most important images in the Bible is the refining of metal. The technique of the day was to heat a crucible full of metal over a fire. Impurities (dross) in the metal rose to the top, and the refiner scraped them off. As the fire was stoked to raise its temperature, more dross rose to the top, and the process was repeated until the refiner could see his face in the molten metal. Sometimes this took up to seven repetitions. David wrote in Psalm 12 that God's words are pure, "as silver tried in a furnace on the earth, refined seven times."

Another psalmist praised God for refining His people as silver is refined (Psalm 66:10). Solomon said "the refining pot is for silver and the furnace for gold, but the LORD tests hearts" (Proverbs 17:3). Both Testaments have many references to this idea.

So God tests the hearts of men, purifying them like a refiner does silver and gold. God's goal is to create a purified people, and He accomplishes this through circumstances that test our faith and require us to exercise it.

God said through Isaiah that He had refined Israel but not as silver because He had used a furnace of affliction (Isaiah 48:10). Peter, speaking of suffering for the sake of the gospel, expressed it this way:

> In this you greatly rejoice, even though now for a little while, if necessary, you have been distressed by various trials, so that the proof of your faith, being more precious than gold which is perishable, even though tested by fire, may be found to result in praise and glory and honor at the revelation of Jesus Christ (1 Peter 1:6-7).

The idea is as clear in the New Testament as it is in the Old: God refines us. He turns up the heat through circumstances in our lives to let the dross rise to the top so He can skim it off, repeating the process throughout our lives until He can see His reflection in us.

The refiner looks at the outer physical appearance of silver or gold, but God looks on the inside, at the heart. Hearts are purified by removing the dross of self-centeredness, worldliness, materialism, and anything else that keeps us from reflecting Jesus perfectly.

Of course, we won't be perfect in this world because of the flesh that is with us so long as we dwell in our earthly bodies, but the refiner's fire includes killing that flesh (1 Corinthians 5:5), and the maturing process continues after death until the day of Jesus Christ (Corinthians 1:8; Philippians 1:6).

God told Israel to clean things fire neither purifies nor destroys by washing them in water, so this refining process clearly does not destroy us but instead improves us. The refiner's fire is different from the fire that tests our works to see which last (1 Corinthians 3:10-15), but neither of these is the fire of the wrath of God that destroys evil. The refiner's fire only purifies us, making us more like Christ.

The refining process is not easy to endure, but in the end it brings greater glory to God. If we sincerely love the Lord and desire His glory, we can persevere in our testing, knowing that it produces what God values most.

Israel's Enemies Will Not Escape

∽∾∽∾

Sometimes the wicked appear to get away with their wickedness and to prosper while the righteous struggle. Justice seems to be ignored. But God is just—He does not let the wicked go unpunished. Israel is the apple of His eye, and those who touch God's people risk His wrath. He will curse those who curse Israel. His judgment is sure.

Day One

This week and next week we will study a new segment in Ezekiel. You'll discover a common thread that weaves through chapters 25–32. We'll begin with our usual process: reading, marking, asking the 5 W's and an H, reading with a purpose.

Read Ezekiel 25, marking key words and phrases from your bookmark. Pay close attention to the nations mentioned, and refer to THE NATIONS OF EZEKIEL'S PROPHECIES in the appendix. List in your notebook what you learn about the judgments on these nations.

Read Numbers 20:14-21, Judges 11:12-28, and Obadiah. These will give you a more complete picture of Israel's relations with Ammon, Moab, and especially Edom.

Finally, determine a theme for Ezekiel 25 and record it on EZEKIEL AT A GLANCE.

Day Two

Read through Ezekiel 26 today, marking key words and phrases from your bookmark. Don't miss the time reference in verse 1. Compare it to the time reference in Ezekiel 24:1 to compare the timing of these prophecies with last week's chapters.

List in your notebook what you learn about the judgment on Tyre.

King Hyram of Tyre helped David prepare for the temple and helped Solomon build it. But things changed. Read Psalm 83 and Isaiah 23:1-12 for more about Tyre's relationship to Israel. Also read Jeremiah 27:1-11.

Determine the theme of Ezekiel 26 and record it on EZE-KIEL AT A GLANCE.

Days Three & Four

Chapter 27 is a longer chapter, so we'll take two days to study it. Read Ezekiel 27 and mark the key words and phrases on your bookmark.

Note what the Lord calls Ezekiel to do. A lamentation is a mourning, a grieving over the loss or destruction of someone or something.

List in your notebook what Tyre says about itself and then make a separate list of what will happen to the city.

Revelation 18 records a lament over another powerful city

with many trading partners. Observe the similarities between these two cities.

As your last assignment for these two days, record a theme for Ezekiel 27 on EZEKIEL AT A GLANCE.

Day Five

We're going to divide our study of Ezekiel 28 into three parts. Today we'll look at verses 1-10. Read Ezekiel 28:1-10 and mark the key words and phrases on your bookmark.

Create a two-column chart in your notebook. In the left column, list bullets about the leader of Tyre (the prince or ruler)—what he says about himself and what is true about him. You'll fill in the other column tomorrow with facts from the rest of the chapter. Also list what God says He will do to this person.

Now, who was addressed in the two previous chapters? Who is addressed in the first ten verses of this chapter? This leader is comparable to Daniel. Read Daniel 1:19-20 and 2:46-49 and note similarities you see.

Who are the strangers (foreigners) who will come against this man? Refresh your memory with Ezekiel 26:7-11 if you can't answer this.

Historians believe the ruler of Tyre at this time was Ethbaal III, whom Nebuchadnezzar (king of Babylon in 573–572 BC) deposed and who died at the hands of the Babylonians.

The phrase "the death of the uncircumcised" is an insult meaning essentially to die in shame. (Read Ezekiel 32:30 for comparison.)

Record a theme for this chapter on EZEKIEL AT A GLANCE.

Day Six

Let's continue our study of Ezekiel 28 today by reading verses 11-19 and marking key words and phrases as usual.

Note the person lamented in verse 12. See what this chapter says about him, and add this information to the list you started yesterday. Now compare this list with yesterday's two-column listings. What is similar and what is different?

Do you think these two persons are the same or different? Why?

Read Isaiah 14:12-21. Do you see any parallels?

Now finish up the chapter by reading Ezekiel 28:20-26, marking key words and phrases as usual. In your notebook, record whom these prophecies are addressed to and what is said about them.

How do the last two verses relate to what is said in chapters 25–28? How do they relate to the chapters before these?

Well, that's it for this week, Beloved! Don't forget to record a theme for Ezekiel 28 on EZEKIEL AT A GLANCE.

Day Seven

 Store in your heart: Ezekiel 28:26

Read and discuss: Ezekiel 25; 26:1-14; 27:1-3,26-36; 28:1-19,25-26

Questions for Discussion or Individual Study

ᴥ Discuss the judgments on Ammon, Moab, Edom, and the Philistines.

∽ Discuss the judgments on Tyre.

∽ What is the connection between the leader of Tyre and the king of Tyre? How are they similar and different? Who is the king of Tyre? Why do you think so?

∽ What is the connection between the judgments you've studied so far and events in the last two verses of chapter 28?

∽ What application can you make this week?

THOUGHT FOR THE WEEK

Solomon wrote, "I have seen everything during my lifetime of futility; there is a righteous man who perishes in his righteousness and there is a wicked man who prolongs his life in his wickedness" (Ecclesiastes 7:15).

Most people probably feel this way when they see injustices, but do the wicked ever ultimately get away with their crimes? Or will justice eventually win out? Surely Ammon, Moab, Edom, Philistia, Tyre, and Sidon thought they could get away with their wickedness toward Israel. Assyria and Babylon did too. Their empires lasted for a long time.

But what happened to these empires? Where are they today? Have they lasted, or were they destroyed? Ezekiel and his fellow exiles knew Assyria had been destroyed, but other nations were still plaguing Judah, gloating over Judah's exile and the siege of Jerusalem. The city and temple were not yet destroyed and the land was not yet desolate, but what did God's prophets predict?

To base our actions only on what makes us feel good or look good in others' eyes will lead to sin. This kind of thinking ignores the negative consequences for our actions and assumes they won't happen to us. The nations in Ezekiel 25–32 followed this sinful thinking pattern. But God's justice includes consequences for all nations, all people. Ignoring God, not believing God, rejecting His law and grace…these are risky behaviors.

What happened to Judah's "older sister"—Israel (the nation), Samaria (the capital city), Oholah (the figurative name)—and what happened to Assyria? God did exactly what He promised to them, so what makes Judah (the nation), Jerusalem (the capital city), Oholibah (the figurative name) think she is exempt? The people think they're exempt because the temple is in Jerusalem, the place where God said He would dwell and always direct His eyes and ears toward. Jeremiah had already tried to convince Judah they were vulnerable, and now Ezekiel is trying.

The naysayers in Judah, pointing to the nations who survive despite their idolatry, say judgment won't come to God's people either. But God says He will judge the nations and judge Judah, and that judgment has already begun. But this apparently will not be convincing. More will be required to convince the people that they can't get away with wickedness. And more is coming. But when?

Ezekiel is faithfully declaring God's word, performing the symbolic acts God directs him to do and going about God's business with endurance. In the middle of it all, his wife dies. Does God excuse him from duty? Surely he needs time to grieve. But what does a watchman need to do? What is his charge? How serious are the consequences for not declaring to the wicked that danger is coming? Ezekiel is on guard duty!

From his behavior, we know Ezekiel believed God was serious and the consequences were critical. In spite of his personal grief, he continued to deliver God's message. He knew that God is just and His judgments are certain. He knew that the wicked don't get away with anything and that God held him responsible to warn them.

God does not want anyone to perish, but for everyone to turn to Him in repentance. And Ezekiel had God's heart on this. Do you? Will you rise to the challenge and keep on in the face of discouragement, fatigue, and difficult personal circumstances? Are you convinced that "building up the wall" and "standing in the gap" is worth the effort?

Do Not Return to Egypt

∾ ∾ ∾ ∾

Soon after Israel left slavery in Egypt, they were tempted to go back. They missed Egypt's fresh food and water, and they seemed willing to trade in their wilderness wandering (which probably seemed like a new slavery) to recover them. Faith was just too tough in the wilderness. Once in the promised land, they asked Egypt for help against their enemies instead of trusting in God—another crisis and difficult test of their faith. But God rules over all nations, raising up kings and nations and destroying them. And God will show Israel why trusting Egypt is the wrong choice.

DAY ONE

The four chapters for this week's study have one thing in common: They are all about judgment on Egypt. Today you'll read Ezekiel 29, marking the key words from your bookmark. Don't miss the time phrase in verse 1. Be sure to compare it to the one in Ezekiel 26:1 and THE RULERS AND PROPHETS OF EZEKIEL'S TIME to see the timing of this chapter. You'll see other time phrases in this chapter and chapters to come, so marking them and keeping track of when the various messages are given will help you see the flow in these four chapters.

Whom does Ezekiel's prophecy address? List items you learn about him in your notebook and then compare this list with your list about the king of Tyre. Note the similarities and differences.

Record the theme of Ezekiel 29 on EZEKIEL AT A GLANCE.

Days Two & Three

Today read Ezekiel 30, marking the key words from your bookmark. Mark the time reference in verse 20 and compare it to the one in Ezekiel 29:1.

Compare Ezekiel 30:2-3 with Joel 1:15 and 2:1-2. Is this the same day or a different one?

Read Deuteronomy 17:14-20, 1 Kings 3:1-3, and 1 Kings 10:26-29. What do you learn about Israel's relationship to Egypt?

Israel's reliance on Egypt continued. Read 2 Kings 17:1-4 and 18:13-24. The Phoenician city-states on the Mediterranean coast—Philistia, Egypt, and Judah—had formed an alliance to resist Assyria. By 2 Kings 18, only Egypt remained of this alliance and it was, as Rabshakeh claimed, as weak as a reed. So it was in no shape to help Israel.

Record the theme of Ezekiel 30 on EZEKIEL AT A GLANCE.

Day Four

The more you read Ezekiel, linger in its message, and meditate on its precepts, the better you will understand your God and His purpose for placing you in this book at this time in your life. Read Ezekiel 31 today, marking the key words from your bookmark. Mark the time reference and compare it to the one in Ezekiel 30:20.

Second Kings 23:28-35 and 24:6-7 also give us background about Egypt and Judah. By this time Egypt had allied with Assyria against the Babylonians, who were becoming the dominant power in the area. Babylon defeated Assyria and Egypt at Carchemish in 605 BC, marking the end of the Assyrian empire. Egypt was weak; Babylon dominated.

Read Daniel 4:10-15,18,20-22,26-27 and compare the verses to Ezekiel 31:3-9. What point does God make in both cases, and how do the two relate?

Record the theme of Ezekiel 31 on EZEKIEL AT A GLANCE.

DAYS FIVE & SIX

Read Ezekiel 32, marking key words from your bookmark as usual. Also mark *uncircumcised,* but don't add it to your bookmark.

Don't miss the time references. Compare them to previous ones and to THE RULERS AND PROPHETS OF EZEKIEL'S TIME.

List what you learn about the uncircumcised nations. Verse 30 is a key to understanding the use of this term in this context.

Record the theme of Ezekiel 32 on EZEKIEL AT A GLANCE.

This week, you've observed four chapters about the judgment of Egypt that may seem unrelated to anything in your life. But before concluding this, consider Israel and Judah's relationship to Egypt. What was wrong with it? What principles are involved that we can apply to ourselves?

What does God think about partial or conditional obedience? About partial or conditional reliance on Him?

Do you need to talk to God about anything in your life?

DAY SEVEN

 Store in your heart: Ezekiel 29:9

Read and discuss: Ezekiel 29; 30:1-12,20-26; 31; 32:1-11,17-23,30-32

QUESTIONS FOR DISCUSSION OR INDIVIDUAL STUDY

- ∞ Discuss what you learned about Egypt's relationships with Israel and Judah.

- ∞ What did you learn about God's demand for obedience?

- ∞ What application to your life can you make from God's judgment on Egypt?

- ∞ Discuss God's use of one nation to judge another.

- ∞ When was Egypt destroyed? Is it all past history or is there a future aspect? Why do you think so?

THOUGHT FOR THE WEEK

Soon after Israel left Egypt, the people wanted to go back. The hard labor in Egypt was difficult, but the food and water there were preferable to the insecurities of uncharted wanderings in a wilderness. The people wanted to take advantage of

Egypt's natural resources instead of depending on the Lord for food from heaven and water from rocks. Slavery to God seemed harder and harsher than slavery to Pharaoh.

That's a pretty good metaphor for us too. All mankind is in slavery to sin and to Satan's kingdom of darkness. God provided a Deliverer-Redeemer for all mankind in His Son, Jesus. Faith in His atoning death and in His resurrection grants us everlasting life, releases us from slavery to sin, and transfers us to His kingdom. The truth of the gospel sets us free.

But life in this kingdom isn't easy. We have trials, temptations, suffering, hardship, attacks by Satan…and these can make us want to return to "Egypt"—to Satan's kingdom.

Satan doesn't apply these pressures in order to get us back—he can't. Once Jesus sets us free, we remain free. Satan wants us to live as if we were still his in order to give those who still belong to him the impression that there's no better alternative, no reason to believe the gospel. And he wants them to think that those who believe the gospel will be miserable and that they would be happier in his kingdom.

Think about it. A life of animal pleasures can be pretty attractive. No one will think you're weird, attack you for being different, or persecute you. You can stay in the mainstream of the world and be like everyone else—normal, according to the world's standards, which accord with the principles of the prince of this world.

Paul explains this in Galatians 5. All you have to do is live in immorality, impurity, enmity, strife, jealousy, angry outbursts, disputes, dissensions, factions, envy, drunkenness, carousing, and things like these. You'll be just like Satan's people. To do these things is easier than to love; to have joy, peace, and patience; to exhibit kindness, goodness, and faithfulness; and to practice gentleness and self-control. That's the lie Satan spreads.

We have to put on God's armor to protect ourselves from Satan's attacks. Satan will send fiery darts of doubt, guilt, and lies. Why should you help others bear their burdens? Your own are hard enough! Why deny yourself? Why humble yourself and consider others before yourself?

The life of faith, life in the Spirit, is not life in the flesh. Flesh and Spirit war against each other just as Satan wars against God. The flesh, the immaterial part of us that prioritizes self above all else, is rooted in the same pride that caused Satan's fall.

But the good news is that we have the Spirit. God has put Him in every believer for the power to say no to fleshly desires and yes to godly living. The Spirit empowers us to live as citizens of heaven. We don't have to yield to the flesh or to Satan's lies. But we must appropriate that power; we must say no to the flesh and to Satan. We aren't puppets. We have willpower, and we must use it to summon the strength Christ provides us to live according to God's demands on us.

We can resist turning back to Egypt. In the end, just as Egypt was destroyed, Satan will be defeated and cast into the lake of fire for eternal punishment, no longer to tempt us. And the flesh will no longer be a source of struggle because the flesh is not part of our glorified natures.

That calls for an *amen!* Rejoice in that glorious truth!

BAD SHEPHERDS, GOOD SHEPHERDS

∾∾∾∾

The prophets often likened rulers in Israel to shepherds because people understood the analogy. Raising sheep was common. Everyone knew what it was like, and everyone knew what shepherds were supposed to do. But unfortunately, most of Israel's leaders (kings and priests) were corrupt. However, God provided His own good shepherd.

DAY ONE

Today read Ezekiel 33:1-20 and mark the key words from your bookmark. Then read Ezekiel 3:17-21 and 18:21-32.

Turn in your notebook to the lists you made from Ezekiel 3 and 18 and compare your items with things you see in Ezekiel 33. You might want to write pertinent facts in parallel columns to see what's similar and what's different.

Now let's think about why so much has been repeated. Look at the chapter themes you've recorded on EZEKIEL AT A GLANCE. What started in Ezekiel 4 that continued through Ezekiel 24? Then, what started in chapter 25 that continued though chapter 32? What is common to both?

Now, what common message do Ezekiel 3 and 33 share,

and how does this message relate to the subject in the intervening chapters?

DAY TWO

Let's finish chapter 33 today. Read Ezekiel 33:21-33, marking key words and phrases from your bookmark. Be sure to mark the time phrase in verse 21 and compare it to previous ones and to THE RULERS AND PROPHETS OF EZEKIEL'S TIME. What did Ezekiel learn in verse 21? When did this happen? From the chart you just referenced, when was the city of Jerusalem taken by the Babylonians?

Now read 2 Kings 25:10-26.

What will happen to the land of Israel according to Ezekiel 33:24-29? Why?

Now think back on the behavior of the people of Judah and Jerusalem before the city fell and the temple was destroyed. What did they say? Read Jeremiah 7:4. What did the people think the temple in Jerusalem protected them from? What did they evidently think about God's word? Did they see it as a blessing or curse? What did they miss?

What principle is taught in verses 30-33? Does this give you any insight into things that happen today? How does this relate to 2 Timothy 4:3-4? How does this teaching challenge you to share truth?

Record the theme of Ezekiel 33 on EZEKIEL AT A GLANCE.

DAY THREE

Read Ezekiel 34:1-22 today and mark the key words and phrases from your bookmark. Mark *shepherds* but don't add it to your bookmark.

Summarize each paragraph in the margins of your Bible or on a separate list.

List in your notebook things you learn about shepherds.

Reread verses 11-16. In what ways is God a good shepherd? Does this invoke any part of Psalm 23?

Reread verses 17-22 and summarize what the Lord says to the sheep.

DAY FOUR

Read Ezekiel 34:23-31 and mark key words and phrases. What verse might be considered a turning point in the chapter and why?

Read Jeremiah 23:1-8; 30:9; and Hosea 3:1-5. What is the implication of these passages?

Record the theme of Ezekiel 34 on EZEKIEL AT A GLANCE.

DAY FIVE

Observe Ezekiel 35, marking key words and phrases from your bookmark.

How does the subject in this chapter shift from that in the preceding one?

What larger geographic area or group of people does Mount Seir represent? Read Genesis 36:8 and Deuteronomy 2:1-5. Have we seen this subject before? Do you recall what the Lord said about Edom? Review day 1 of week 8 on page 65.

List in your notebook things you learn about Edom in Ezekiel 35. What will the Edomites know and why?

Record the theme of Ezekiel 35 on EZEKIEL AT A GLANCE.

DAY SIX

Today's study will be a little unique. Instead of observing a chapter or part of a chapter, we'll review to set the stage for next week. Besides, after studying 35 chapters of Ezekiel, you may be ready for a change of pace! So let's start our recap at the beginning. Who is Ezekiel, where is he, and what does God call him to do?

When in Israel's history does Ezekiel live? Who is reigning where, what year is it, and what has happened with regard to Babylon?

What is the first thing that happens to Ezekiel? What does he see and hear?

What kinds of things is Ezekiel asked to do and why?

What has Israel been doing, and what does God say He will do in response?

What does Ezekiel see in the temple?

What kind of behavior does God ascribe to Israel? What analogies does He use?

What does God say about the nations around Israel? List the nations, describe the way they have acted toward Israel, and review the consequences of their actions.

How much time has passed in all these chapters? Where do these chapters fit in the history of Babylon and of Jerusalem?

Now, what is the message in this week's chapters? What seems to be in store for Israel next? In other words, if there *is* a turning point, where does it start, and what kinds of things do you expect in coming chapters?

DAY SEVEN

Store in your heart: Ezekiel 34:23
Read and discuss: Ezekiel 33–35

QUESTIONS FOR DISCUSSION OR INDIVIDUAL STUDY

∽ Review what you've learned in Ezekiel so far. Discuss the flow of events in Ezekiel's experience, visions, signs, messages, audiences, personal life, and so on.

∽ How does Ezekiel describe Israel's future?

∽ Discuss a phrase you have seen throughout the book that ties together the message so far.

∽ What principles should the nations know?

∽ What lessons for your life have you learned so far in Ezekiel?

THOUGHT FOR THE WEEK

"The LORD is my shepherd, I shall not want." These comforting words are familiar to many. And comfort is needed when times are hard, when life seems overwhelming, when everything around you seems to be crumbling.

Think about Jerusalem in Ezekiel's day. The leaders of the nation, the shepherds, had been reassuring their people, telling them everything was going to be all right, that God wouldn't abandon His temple, city, or people to destruction and captivity. After all, He promised the land to them forever and said He would always be attentive to Jerusalem and the temple.

But prophets like Jeremiah and Ezekiel had a different

message. Jeremiah remained in Jerusalem, delivering God's message to the people there. Ezekiel was taken into captivity and delivered God's message to the people there. Both men proclaimed the truth when others were falsely predicting that the captivity was almost over and that the people would soon return to Judah.

These unfaithful shepherds, princes, priests, and prophets were not speaking for God. In fact, they led the people into idolatry. They were about as far from God's truth as anyone could be. They led the sheep astray and to destruction rather than to green pastures and still waters.

David had been a shepherd as a youth. The imagery of a good shepherd caring for his flock makes Psalm 23 easy to understand. He knew how to be a good shepherd to sheep. According to Ezekiel 34:23-24, he will once again shepherd God's people, feeding them His truth.

Jesus, the descendant of David, used the same imagery. He called Himself the good shepherd who lays down His life for the sheep. He said He knows His own sheep and they know Him and recognize His voice.

The people in Ezekiel's days did not know God's voice. Shepherds claimed to bring messages from God, and when God's true prophets brought a contradictory message, the people couldn't distinguish between the truth and the lie. That's because they were so far from God, they didn't recognize His voice when they heard it. Processing words of peace and safety is easier and more comforting than processing words of danger and destruction.

Deuteronomy provides a simple test for the validity of a prophet: If what he prophesied didn't come to pass, he was false. If it came to pass but he directed hearts away from the Lord, he was equally false. Only if a prophet spoke fully for God, not just prophetic truth but all truth, was he true.

In Ezekiel 33:33, God says to Ezekiel, "So when it comes to

pass—as surely it will—then they will know that a prophet has been in their midst." Ezekiel will be vindicated. The destruction had already occurred. Now the message will turn to restoration—return from exile and reinstatement of David as shepherd. As we look to future chapters, what other promises will come to pass to show that God has truly spoken through Ezekiel?

THE NEW COVENANT

God is a covenant-keeping God. He made a covenant with Noah, another one with Abraham, another one (through Moses) with Israel as a nation at Mount Sinai, and another one with David. And about the time of Ezekiel's ministry in Babylon, God promised through Jeremiah that He would make yet another covenant:

> "Behold, days are coming," declares the LORD, "when I will make a new covenant with the house of Israel and with the house of Judah, not like the covenant which I made with their fathers in the day I took them by the hand to bring them out of the land of Egypt, My covenant which they broke, although I was a husband to them," declares the LORD (Jeremiah 31:31-32).

DAY ONE

Read Ezekiel 36:1-21 today, marking key words and phrases from your bookmark. Also mark *I will*, *jealousy*,[5] and *insults*,[6] but don't add them to your bookmark. Don't miss contrasts introduced by *but,* and don't miss conclusions introduced by *therefore.* Keep track of the flow of thought.

Identify the recipient of the prophecy. Then make a two-column list in your notebook. On one side, record what you think has been fulfilled. On the other side, record what you think remains ahead and why.

List the *I will*'s in verses 9-15. You'll see another list of these tomorrow.

Were God's prior actions just? Did Israel deserve judgment? Conversely, why is God going to do what He promises?

DAY TWO

Let's continue our study of Ezekiel 36 today. Read Ezekiel 36:22-38, marking key words and phrases from your bookmark and any new ones you see in this part of the chapter.

Note who this part of the chapter addresses in contrast to the first part. Why is God about to act? Compare the reason in verses 22-23 with the reason in verse 21.

From the *I will*'s starting in verse 24, what will God do when He proves Himself holy among Israel in the sight of the nations?

Now compare Ezekiel 36:24-28 with these cross-references:

> Jeremiah 31:31-34
>
> Luke 22:1,7-8,14-20
>
> Hebrews 8:6-13
>
> Hebrews 9:11-22

So who is included in this new covenant promised to Israel and Jacob? Read Ephesians 2:11-18. Is the promise still valid for Israel? Read Romans 11:1-2, 11-12, and 25-29.

What things will God do "moreover"? (The word appears twice in the second part of chapter 36.) Why will God do all this? Who will benefit and in what ways?

Finally today, record the theme of Ezekiel 36 on EZEKIEL AT A GLANCE.

DAY THREE

Read Ezekiel 37, marking key words as usual. Mark *bones* and *stick* but don't add them to your bookmark.

This chapter is familiar to many who have sung, "Dem bones, dem bones, dem dry bones…" But the song focuses only on the physical connections of the bones, not the meaning behind the metaphor, and it doesn't address the two sticks or their metaphorical meaning.

List in your notebook what you learn about the bones and the sticks. What information did you learn from the sticks that wasn't crystal clear from the metaphor of the bones?

What did you learn about David from this chapter? Compare it to Ezekiel 34:23-24.

Read the following passages and then compile what you learn about David's future:

> Isaiah 9:1-7
>
> Jeremiah 23:5-8
>
> Jeremiah 30:1-9
>
> Jeremiah 33:15-16
>
> Hosea 3:1-5
>
> Amos 9:11-12

Don't miss the nugget about the covenant. Read Hebrews 13:20.

Finally, record the theme of Ezekiel 37 on EZEKIEL AT A GLANCE.

DAY FOUR

Read Ezekiel 38, marking key words and phrases as usual. Chapters 38 and 39 address a common subject. Note his name. Don't forget to double underline geographical locations and mark references to time.

Refer to THE NATIONS OF EZEKIEL 38 AND 39 in the appendix to see where the nations mentioned are located.

List what you learn about what Gog and the nations will do. When will this happen? What will the conditions in Israel be? This is key to identifying when this occurs.

What will God do "in that day" to the armies of Gog?

Read Revelation 20:1-10, which also mentions Gog. When does God attack there? Before you jump to any conclusions, you should know there are differing opinions, and remember, we've got more study ahead of us. This is just to stimulate your thinking!

Record the theme of Ezekiel 38 on EZEKIEL AT A GLANCE.

DAY FIVE

Read Ezekiel 39:1-16, marking key words and phrases from your bookmark. Be sure to mark time phrases and geographical locations.

List what you learn about the slaughter. Who will be involved, and who will know about God?

Also list what you learn about the cleanup afterward. How

long will it take to burn up the weapons? How long will it take to bury the dead? Where will the burial ground be, and what will it be called? What is its purpose?

For comparison, these other Bible passages describe end-times battles and great destruction: Joel 3:9-14; Zechariah 12–14; and Revelation 14:17-20; 16:12-16; 19:1-16.

DAY SIX

Finish Ezekiel 39, reading verses 17-29 and marking key words and phrases from your bookmark. Include time phrases and geographical locations.

List in your notebook facts about the feast for the birds and beasts. Read the description in Revelation 19:17-21 of another feast for birds. Without equating the two battles, compare the sizes of the slaughters and the aftermaths. Then list what happens after the feast. Who will know what?

Don't miss the reference to the Spirit in the last verse of Ezekiel 39. How does this relate to chapter 36?

Now, you're probably wondering when this battle of Gog and the land of Magog will take place. Does it occur after the millennium (as it's described in Revelation 20), or does it occur another time?

Consider the conditions in Israel before this event in Ezekiel happens. How are they living? What are the city fortifications like? What happens in verses 22 and 25-29? Is this consistent with conditions in the millennium in Revelation 20?

Bible teachers vary on their understanding of when this event in Ezekiel occurs. The subject is too difficult to handle in one day's work in this series, so we urge you to do further study.

Finally for today and this week, record the theme of Ezekiel 39 on EZEKIEL AT A GLANCE.

Day Seven

Store in your heart: Ezekiel 36:26-27

Read and discuss: Jeremiah 31:31-34; Ezekiel 36:7-15,22-29; 37; 38:10-16; 39

Questions for Discussion or Individual Study

∾ Discuss your insights about the new covenant. How is it different from the covenant of the Law, the old covenant?

∾ Discuss implications of the metaphors of the bones and the sticks. How does your previous study of Israel fit these metaphors?

∾ Discuss the battle of Gog and Magog. Cover all the who, what, when, where, why, and how questions as they apply.

∾ What life lessons can you draw from this week's study?

Thought for the Week

The writer of Hebrews gives us a great perspective on the new covenant God promised Israel. His letter to the Hebrews explains why the new covenant is better than the old covenant (the Law), which God made with Israel at Mount Sinai. As Jeremiah explains, Israel broke that covenant.

The writer of Hebrews explains that this covenant is based on a better promise, a better sacrifice with better blood, and a better high priest than the covenant of the Law. Jesus is the better sacrifice; His blood is better than the blood of bulls and goats. His sacrifice was once for all, not day after day, year after year. His blood is better because He is like us, made man to identify with us. And unlike the goat that took on the people's sins for the sanctification of the flesh (Hebrews 9:13), Jesus actually became sin for us "so that we might become the righteousness of God in Him" (2 Corinthians 5:21).

The author of Hebrews also tells us that God takes away the first (the old covenant) to establish the second (the new covenant), making the old covenant obsolete. In Paul's letter to the Galatians, he explained the purpose of the Law (the old covenant): "The Law has become our tutor to lead us to Christ, that we might be justified by faith. But now that faith has come, we are no longer under a tutor" (Galatians 3:24-25).

Among the benefits of this new covenant are a new heart and a new spirit in us. God removes hearts of stone and replaces them with hearts of flesh, and He puts His Spirit within.

Jesus is the better high priest also because His priesthood is not like Aaron's temporary priesthood but rather like Melchizedek's perpetual one. Jeremiah and Ezekiel prophesy that God will make this new covenant with Israel and Judah. Can anyone else participate in this new covenant? The good news is, yes we can!

On the night Jesus was betrayed, He ate the Passover with His disciples and instituted what we call the Lord's Supper. He took the cup after the meal and said, "This cup which is poured out for you is the new covenant in My blood" (Luke 22:20). The apostle Paul expanded this message to the church in Corinth: "This cup is the new covenant in My blood; do this, as often as you drink it, in remembrance of Me" (1 Corinthians 11:25). This conclusively extends the new covenant to Gentiles—anyone who believes the gospel.

So "there is neither Jew nor Greek [Gentile]—you are all one in Christ Jesus" (Galatians 3:28). Rejoice in the new covenant, Beloved. Rejoice in it!

THE TEMPLE
OF THE LORD

∾∾∾∾

God destroyed the temple of Solomon, a building dedicated to worshipping God that had degenerated to a place for worshipping everything but God. Judah trusted this temple to save them from Babylon, but it didn't. Now God promised a new temple, not like the one Solomon built. What will it look like?

∾∾∾
DAYS ONE & TWO

This week starts a new segment in Ezekiel, as you'll see by the change in subject. Ezekiel 40 is long, so we'll take two days to digest it. Read the chapter and mark the key words and phrases from your bookmark. You'll notice that most of the words on your bookmark are not used much because the subject changes. Mark the locations where Ezekiel was taken. If you find it helpful, mark the phrase *brought me.*[7] The vision continues for several chapters, so you can add this to your bookmark if you choose to mark it. Also mark the time reference in verse 1 and compare it to the others and to THE RULERS AND PROPHETS OF EZEKIEL'S TIME.

What event occurs in this chapter? When was the previous

vision? What has been the subject in all the other chapters? What is the subject in chapter 40?

Review what happened in the temple in Ezekiel 8–11. Read 2 Kings 25:1-3 and 2 Chronicles 36:11-21. From the historical cross-references in Kings and Chronicles and THE RULERS AND PROPHETS OF EZEKIEL'S TIME, what happened to the temple in 586 BC?

Now, what event is the man in chapter 40 showing Ezekiel? When will the fulfillment of this vision occur? Does the text tell us or give any hints?

List what Ezekiel sees. If you think you'll learn best by sketching the vision, do it. (We have included three diagrams in the appendix.)

Record the theme of Ezekiel 40 on EZEKIEL AT A GLANCE.

DAY THREE

Continuing the vision, read Ezekiel 41, marking key words and phrases from your bookmark as usual. Refer to the diagrams in the appendix or continue sketching what you read.

For a comparison to Solomon's temple, read 1 Kings 6 and 2 Chronicles 3. Compare these Old Testament temples to the temple the New Testament describes:

1 Corinthians 3:10-17

1 Corinthians 6:12-20

2 Corinthians 6:14-18

Ephesians 2:19-22

1 Peter 2:4-10

Record the theme of Ezekiel 41 on EZEKIEL AT A GLANCE.

Day Four

As you observe Ezekiel 42, mark the key words and phrases from your bookmark.

Record the theme of Ezekiel 42 on EZEKIEL AT A GLANCE.

Days Five & Six

Ezekiel 43 is not a long chapter, but we'll take two days to study it because a good break in the narrative follows it and because we have many significant cross-references to consider.

Read Ezekiel 43, marking key words and phrases from your bookmark as usual. Refer to the sketch of the altar in the appendix or draw your own.

Now list in your notebook what you learn about the glory of the Lord.

Compare the visions Ezekiel refers to in verse 3.

Review what you learned about the glory of the Lord from week 3 (Ezekiel 8–11).

Read Haggai 2:1-9; 2 Chronicles 5–7; and 1 Kings 8. Take notes concerning the glory of the Lord and what God says about Jerusalem, the temple, idolatry, returning to Him, and the like.

Read Leviticus 9 and compare the dedication with those in 1 Kings, 2 Chronicles, and Ezekiel.

Record a theme for Ezekiel 43 on EZEKIEL AT A GLANCE.

DAY SEVEN

Store in your heart: Ezekiel 43:7

Read and discuss: Ezekiel 40:1-4; 43; and the cross-references we suggested.

QUESTIONS FOR DISCUSSION OR INDIVIDUAL STUDY

- Discuss Ezekiel's vision. Compare the dimensions of this temple with those of the tabernacle and the two previous temples.

- Discuss the glory of the Lord leaving and returning to the temple. Compare its presence in the tabernacle, the temple Solomon built, the temple Zerubbabel built, and the temple Ezekiel saw in his vision.

- What did God call Ezekiel to do with this vision?

- Compare the dedications of Solomon's and Ezekiel's temples.

- Compare these temples to God's temple that is not made with human hands. What applications can you make to your life?

THOUGHT FOR THE WEEK

"The temple of the LORD!" was the cry of the people when Babylon was besieging Jerusalem. They were convinced that God would not abandon His temple to destruction. They were wrong. They did not believe their abominations caused the judgment God promised. They believed only promises of blessing, such as the promise of God's continued presence in the temple.

Ezekiel was given a vision of another temple, a much larger one than the one Solomon built and Babylon destroyed in 586 BC. It was also much larger than the one Zerubbabel built, Herod greatly enlarged and made more ornate, and Rome destroyed in AD 70. The temple in Ezekiel's vision would be used by priests making sacrifices, as did its predecessors. But was it the final temple?

God revealed through Paul and Peter that earthly temples made of stones and erected by human hands are only a picture of the real temple God dwells in today—His church—in which we are living stones, Jesus Christ being the cornerstone. We are built on the foundation of the apostles and prophets. We are the spiritual temple God dwells in through the person of the Holy Spirit, and we are also the priests who offer spiritual sacrifices to Him.

When we compare the two kinds of temples, we see how precisely God described the temple Ezekiel saw in his vision. God is concerned with details; in fact, He goes into incredible detail describing what living stones in God's spiritual house of worship look like. The four Gospels describe Jesus, the cornerstone. The Gospels and Acts describe the apostles, and the Old Testament describes the prophets. These are our foundation. Their teachings are what we build our lives on.

Consider Ezekiel's obedience and hardship. In the midst of all God gave him to do, God took away the delight of his eyes (his wife), but Ezekiel continued to deliver his message. The people rejected his message, but he continued to be obedient to God by preaching.

Does God call us to be any different? No, He calls us to be silver, gold, and precious stones that stand after the refiner's fire. He calls us to leave behind the works that are no more permanent than wood, hay, and straw. He gives us explicit commands concerning holy living and being a royal priesthood, a holy nation, a people for His own possession, so that we may proclaim the excellencies of Him who called us out of darkness and into His marvelous light (1 Peter 2:9). God gives details of how to live to accomplish His purpose in us. So, unlike the Israelites who in Ezekiel's day didn't study and obey God's Word, we need to know these details for godly living if we are to stand the refiner's fire. We need to know how to be that priesthood and how to offer spiritual sacrifices (our lives) for the cause of Christ.

Make this a conscientious goal as you reflect on the temple of God and His glory that fills it. Remember, you are the temple of God today, and He fills you with His Spirit.

THE PROMISED LAND

❧❧❧❧

God promised a land to Abraham and his descendants. He kept that promise, passing it to Isaac and Jacob (Israel). After Jacob's family went to Egypt and became a nation, God returned the people to the land and distributed portions by lot to the 12 tribes of Israel, the descendants of Jacob. God promised long life on the land if they obeyed and expulsion from the land if they disobeyed and worshipped other gods. He kept His promise and removed them from the land, using Assyria and Babylon to take them captive. But God promised to bring back Israel and Judah. When He keeps that promise, things aren't the same; they're different.

DAY ONE

Read Ezekiel 44, marking key words and phrases from your bookmark as usual. List the priests' responsibilities and note who among Aaron's descendants will minister before God.

Compare the following with Ezekiel 44 and note what you learn:

Exodus 28:40-43

Exodus 29:9,42-46

Leviticus 10:8-10

Leviticus 21:1-13

Deuteronomy 17:8-9

There are many other passages we could look at that describe the priests and their duties, but these should be enough to show where the commands in Ezekiel come from.

Record the theme of Ezekiel 44 on EZEKIEL AT A GLANCE.

DAY TWO

Read Ezekiel 45 and mark key words and phrases. List what will be done for and by the princes.

Read Leviticus 23 and compare the feasts in Ezekiel 45:18-25. Note any differences. If you have time and are interested, compare the offerings in Leviticus 1–5 with the ones in Ezekiel 45:13-17.

Finally today, record the theme of Ezekiel 45 on EZEKIEL AT A GLANCE.

DAY THREE

Read through Ezekiel 46 and mark key words and phrases as usual. List the responsibilities of the prince. You won't find parallel passages in the Pentateuch because the Mosaic Law prescribed no earthly king or prince over the people of Israel. God was their king. Only later did God concede the king they demanded.

Read Deuteronomy 17:14-20 and 1 Samuel 15. Saul was the first king of Israel, and his reign was a disaster. For the most part, the kings after him were much like him. David was exceptionally good but not perfect, and his son Solomon married many foreign wives who turned his heart away from God to their idols. Subsequently, all the kings of the northern kingdom (Israel) and most of the kings of the southern kingdom (Judah) strayed from the commandments of the Lord.

Finally, record the theme of Ezekiel 46 on EZEKIEL AT A GLANCE.

DAY FOUR

Read Ezekiel 47 and mark key words and phrases as usual. Mark *inherit(ance)* but don't add it to your bookmark. Also mark locations.

List the boundaries of the land. Compare these with the boundaries in Genesis 15:18-21 and Exodus 23:31. You can also study the boundaries in Joshua 13–19, which we'll look at tomorrow when we study each tribe's boundaries.

Record the theme of Ezekiel 47 on EZEKIEL AT A GLANCE.

DAY FIVE

Read Ezekiel 48 and mark the chapter as usual.

God not only gave specifics for the temple, the altar, and the sacrifices, but also apportioned the land. Refer to THE TRIBES, THE PRINCE'S PORTION, THE CITY, THE SANCTUARY in the appendix or make your own sketch for the tribal inheritances.

Read Joshua 13–19 and take notes about the location of each tribe's inheritance. Refer to the map titled JOSHUA: OCCUPYING THE PROMISED LAND in the appendix.

One of the most significant phrases in this chapter is in verse 35, where the city is called *Jehovah Shammah* (the Lord [is] there). Given all you've seen about the glory of the Lord in Ezekiel, meditate on the meaning of that name for the city.

Record the theme of Ezekiel 48 on EZEKIEL AT A GLANCE.

DAY SIX

Finally, Beloved, we come to the end of our study. We've looked at all 48 chapters, and now it's time to pull it all together. On the one hand, it's exciting to get to the end of such a long book. On the other, it's sad that our time together in this glorious book has come to an end. But what a privilege it has been to explore Ezekiel together with you. I'm sure many verses will remain with you forever. And although we don't understand everything in Ezekiel, we can stand firmly on those things we do understand, so rejoice.

Now turn to EZEKIEL AT A GLANCE. If you've entered chapter themes as we've suggested these 13 weeks, your chart is almost complete. You know the author and can add his name. You know the dates in the book from THE RULERS AND PROPHETS OF EZEKIEL'S TIME. You know the purpose of the book from the visions Ezekiel received and the messages he delivered. You may want to take some time to think about a concise way to state this purpose and then fill in these elements of your chart.

Another item you haven't filled in yet is the theme of the book. This is an overarching statement of the book's message and purpose. We've seen key repeated words and phrases throughout the book, not in just one or in a few chapters, and these convey main ideas in the book too. So take some time and think about how you want to express the main idea of the whole book.

The last things to fill in are the columns called "segment divisions." These are provided so you can identify sections (sometimes as broad as several chapters) that cover a specific topic. We've mentioned several new segments over the last 13 weeks. If you didn't mark them then, now is the time. This will really help you solidify your understanding of the book's structure.

New segments begin in many ways. Sometimes they're set off by new content (such as a prophetic message), sometimes by a new audience, sometimes by a new time reference, and sometimes by a shift in geography. You've seen all of these. You might want to note these kinds of segmentations on the chart in one of the columns. Those are examples, and you may find more and different ways to segment the book. But thinking through all the chapters and reviewing all the content is a great way to review and wrap up. Enjoy!

Day Seven

 Store in your heart: Ezekiel 48:35b

Read and discuss: Ezekiel 44–48 (You choose the portions to read; don't read every verse.)

Questions for Discussion or Individual Study

- ∾ Discuss all you've learned about the princes and their offerings.

- ∾ What did you learn about the boundaries of the land and each tribe's inheritance? What is similar and what is different from the inheritances in Joshua?

- ∾ What did you learn about the city, the sanctuary, and the princes' and leaders' portions?

- ∿ Discuss the theme and structure (segments) of the book.

- ∿ What principles did you learn over the past 13 weeks that you can apply to your life? Leave plenty of time for discussion and wrap-up.

THOUGHT FOR THE WEEK

From the time of God's covenant to Abraham, the promised land figured prominently in God's encouragements and warnings to His people. In Genesis, you can trace this promise to Abraham (12:1-3; 13:14-17; 15:1-21; 17:1-8), Isaac (17:19; 21:10; 24:7; 25:5; 26:3), and Jacob (28:13-14; 46:2-4).

As you'll recall, the boundaries are set out in Scripture as well. These boundaries are close to the boundaries of the modern state of Israel. One salient feature of the promise to Abraham is that ownership is forever. Another is that the land passes to Abraham's son Isaac, not Ishmael, and to Isaac's son Jacob (whose name was changed to Israel), not Esau. Finally, God told Abraham and his descendants never to sell the land.

Old Testament history records, however, that foreign powers invaded the land and expelled the Israelites (called "Jews" after the Babylonian captivity because they were the remnant of Judah). After these invasions, various other people lived in the land and claimed ownership for their families for hundreds of years.

After World War II and the slaughter of six million Jews in the Nazi Holocaust, the United Nations voted to establish a permanent homeland for the Jews in what was at that time called Palestine. *Palestine* is the English form of the name the Roman emperor Hadrian gave the land after the Bar Kochba revolt in AD 135. He changed the name of the Roman province of Judea (the Latin transliteration of Judah) to Syria-Palestina—"Syria of the Philistines." The name Palestine stuck from that time on. After driving out the Ottoman Turks in World War I, Great Britain was given a mandate to rule Palestine, which was mostly occupied by Arabs. Jews had been returning since the late nineteenth century, but the United Nations' decision established a legal entity, a nation called Israel, on the land God promised Abraham.

Today, numerous controversies exist: Who should live where in the region? Who should govern? Should there be one or two states? Where should the capital be? We know the Bible says whose land it is—whom God gave it to. We also know that in the end, according to Ezekiel, it will be Israel's once more despite the discord we see today.

If we have to choose sides—God's or man's—whose do we choose? What happened to Judah when they turned their backs on God's Word? What did God say to Abraham in Genesis 12? "I will bless those who bless you, and the one who curses you I will curse. And in you all the families of the earth will be blessed" (Genesis 12:3).

All families of the earth have already been blessed. Jesus, the promised seed of Adam through Abraham, Isaac, Jacob, and Judah, has provided redemption from the penalty of sin. He has provided a way for us to be free from the slavery to sin now and one day to be free from its presence altogether.

Appendix

THE RULERS AND PROPHETS OF EZEKIEL'S TIME

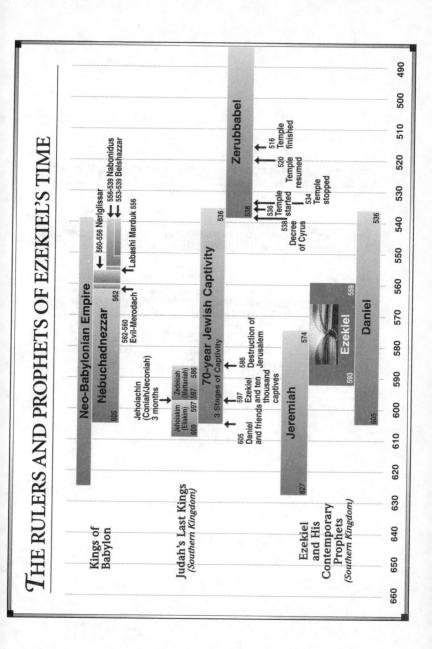

The Jewish Calendar

Babylonian names (B) for the months are still used today for the Jewish calendar. Canaanite names (C) were used prior to the Babylonian captivity in 586 B.C. Four are mentioned in the Old Testament. **Adar-Sheni** is an intercalary month used every two to three years or seven times in 19 years.

1st month	2nd month	3rd month	4th month
Nisan (B) Abib (C) March-April	Iyyar (B) Ziv (C) April-May	Sivan (B) May-June	Tammuz (B) June-July
7th month	*8th month*	*9th month*	*10th month*
5th month	**6th month**	**7th month**	**8th month**
Ab (B) July-August	Elul (B) August-September	Tishri (B) Ethanim (C) September-October	Marcheshvan (B) Bul (C) October-November
11th month	*12th month*	*1st month*	*2nd month*
9th month	**10th month**	**11th month**	**12th month**
Chislev (B) November-December	Tebeth (B) December-January	Shebat (B) January-February	Adar (B) February-March
3rd month	*4th month*	*5th month*	*6th month*

Sacred calendar appears in black • Civil calendar appears in gray

EXILES OF JUDAH TO BABYLON

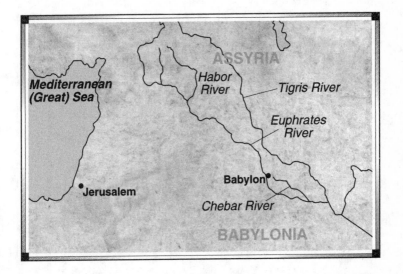

SOLOMON'S TEMPLE

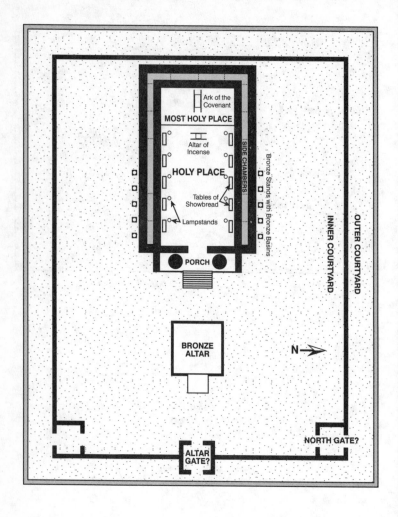

The Nations of Ezekiel's Prophecies

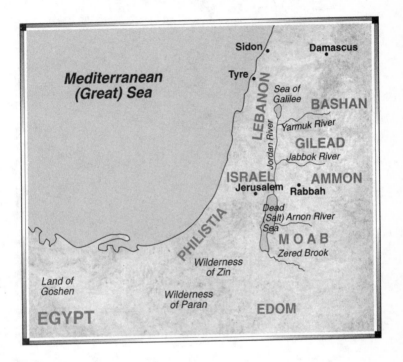

THE NATIONS OF EZEKIEL 38 AND 39

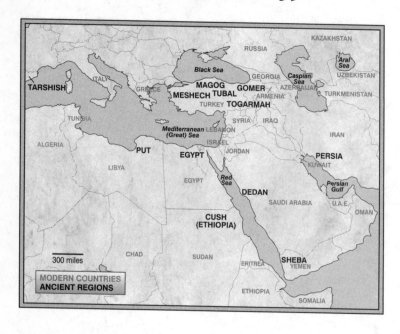

THE GATES OF EZEKIEL'S TEMPLE

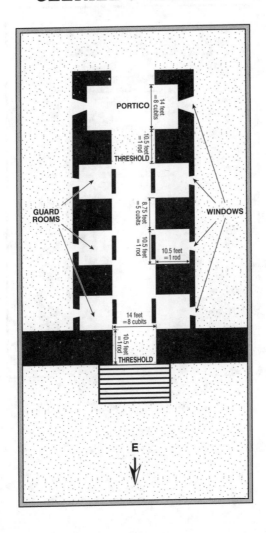

PORTICO

14 feet = 8 cubits

10.5 feet = 1 rod

THRESHOLD

GUARD ROOMS

WINDOWS

8.75 feet = 5 cubits

10.5 feet = 1 rod

10.5 feet = 1 rod

14 feet = 8 cubits

10.5 feet = 1 rod

THRESHOLD

E

EZEKIEL'S TEMPLE

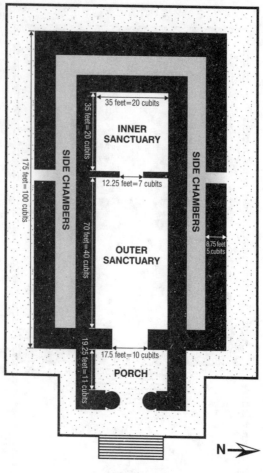

For Ezekiel's Temple
1 cubit = 1.75 ft.
i.e., 1 cubit + a handbreath (Ez. 40:5)

THE ALTAR

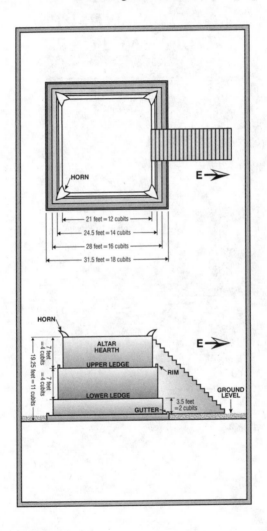

THE TRIBES, THE PRINCES' PORTION, THE CITY, THE SANCTUARY

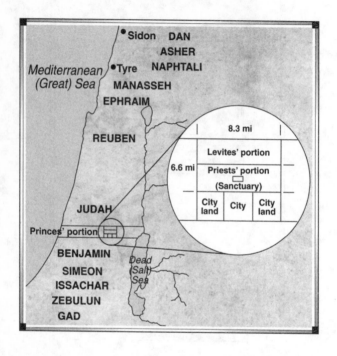

JOSHUA: OCCUPYING THE PROMISED LAND

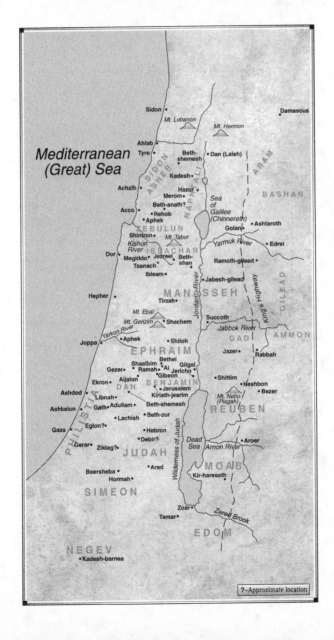

EZEKIEL AT A GLANCE

Theme of Ezekiel:

Author:

SEGMENT DIVISIONS

Date:

Purpose:

Key Words:

the word of the Lord

prophesy

son of man

covenant

vision(s)

the glory of God (the Lord)

Spirit (spirit)

know that I am the Lord

iniquity (sin, abominations)

rebelled (rebellious)

sword

wrath

mountain(s)

heart

harlot (harlotries, adultery)

blood

sanctuary (temple)

the day of the Lord

		CHAPTER THEMES
		1
		2
		3
		4
		5
		6
		7
		8
		9
		10
		11
		12
		13
		14
		15
		16
		17
		18
		19
		20
		21
		22
		23
		24

EZEKIEL AT A GLANCE

SEGMENT DIVISIONS

		CHAPTER THEMES
		25
		26
		27
		28
		29
		30
		31
		32
		33
		34
		35
		36
		37
		38
		39
		40
		41
		42
		43
		44
		45
		46
		47
		48

Notes

❧❧❧❧❧

1. KJV, NKJV, ESV: hear
2. NIV, ESV: some
3. NIV: prostitutes; ESV: whores
4. KJV, NKJV: lawful; NIV, ESV: just
5. NIV: zeal
6. KJV, NKJV: shame; NIV: scorn; ESV: reproach
7. NKJV, NIV: took me

Books in the
New Inductive Study Series

❧❧❧❧

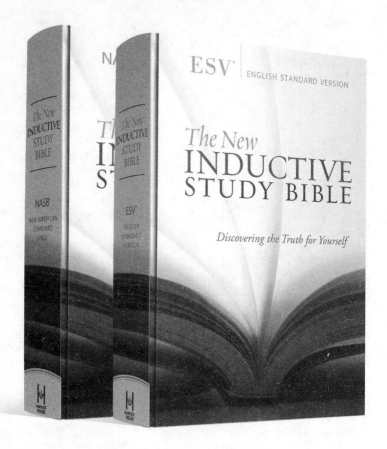

Harvest House Books by Kay Arthur

∞∞∞∞

∞∞∞

Discover 4 Yourself® Inductive Bible Studies for Kids

Do you want a life that thrives?

Wherever you are on your spiritual journey, there is a way to discover Truth for yourself so you can find the abundant life in Christ.

Kay Arthur and Pete De Lacy invite you to join them on the ultimate journey. Learn to live life God's way by knowing Him through His Word.

Visit www.precept.org/thrives to take the next step by downloading a free study tool.

PRECEPT MINISTRIES INTERNATIONAL
THE INDUCTIVE BIBLE STUDY PEOPLE